CONSTANT SHOTGUN
A Cold War Memoir

By Colonel Glenn R. Whicker, USAF (Retired)

Copyright © 2025 Glenn R. Whicker

Published by Whickstone Enterprises
All rights reserved.
Published in the United States of America

ISBN: 978-0-9996402-4-1

Cover design: Addie Harward. Adapted from an original flight suit patch created by Al Westrom.

Pen-and-ink drawings created by Jeff Bushman of Family Histories Illustrated.

All photographs were taken by the author with the following exceptions, sourced as follows:

Page 63 - https://en.wikipedia.org/wiki/Ilyushin_Il-76
Page 64 - https://en.wikipedia.org/wiki/ZIL-4104
Page 87 - https://en.wikipedia.org/wiki/Antonov_An-225_Mriya
Page 170 - Generated using Microsoft Flight Simulator
Pages 216-217 - Photos by Al Westrom
Page 228 - Photo taken by Soviet crewmember
Page 232 - TSgt. David S. Nolan, Airman Magazine, July 1992
Page 262 - Washington Post photographer, date unknown

Acknowledgements:

I want to acknowledge the help of Elizabeth Thomas of Stories From The Hearth. Her editing expertise has been invaluable.

Special thanks as well to Alan Westrom and Charles Miller for fact-checking my sometimes murky memory of these events.

*Dedicated to my eternal companion, Pam.
An aircraft, after all, is merely a means of transport.
What it conveys makes all the difference. In our relationship,
airplanes carried our love, our family, and our destiny
as precious cargo from one assignment to another.
I am grateful that, as my co-pilot, she has always stuck with me
as we navigate the uncharted territory of life together.*

*To my daughters,
who were unaware of their dad's escapades throughout
their formative years, but who benefited from it all.*

*To my grandchildren,
who never experienced the realities of the Cold War.
May these stories help them understand the value
of the freedoms they enjoy.*

CONTENTS

A Pilot's Note 1
Chapter 1: First Glance 5
Chapter 2: Slow Go 11
Chapter 3: The Call 17
Chapter 4: Gander 25
Chapter 5: Song of Peace 33
Chapter 6: Candid 41
Chapter 7: José Martí 47
Chapter 8: La Habana 53
Chapter 9: The Flag 61
Chapter 10: The General 71
Chapter 11: Stone Cold 77
Chapter 12: The World's Largest Aircraft 87
Chapter 13: Children of Chernobyl 99
Chapter 14: Coup d'Etat 107
Chapter 15: Reversal 117
Chapter 16: Reborn! 127
Chapter 17: Wrong Airport 141
Chapter 18: Wasted Runway 159
Chapter 19: Engine Lost! 173
Chapter 20: Sentenced to Siberia 185
Chapter 21: First-Class and Evergreen 197
Chapter 22: Anadyr & the Bomber 209
Chapter 23: Bear N' the Buff 223
Chapter 24: Boris Meets Stone 235
Conclusion 247

TECH TABS

#1 – Why Become a Pilot? 6-7
#2 – Pressurization 84-85
#3 – Destruction of the AN-225 96-97
#4 – Flight Pubs 124-125
#5 – Transponders 138-139
#6 – "Spatial D" at Home 142-143
#7 – Runway Names 152-153

#8 – Weather Minima 160-161
#9 – Flying the Condor 226-227

APPENDIX 251
    ONE: First Flight - Westrom 251
    TWO: Emergency Comms - Westrom 257
    THREE: Helicopter Babushkas - Todorov 264
    FOUR: Anadyr Friendship - Trecziak 267
    FIVE: Double Dual-Engine Flameout - Miller 269
    SIX: Hurricane Gloria & KGB Poison - Peluso 274

GLOSSARY & ACRONYMS 277

Примечание Пилота
"A Pilot's Note"

CONSTANT SHOTGUN

*Mission: To provide Russian-speaking
USAF pilots or navigators as onboard escorts
to assist foreign crews entering or departing
United States airspace in Soviet aircraft
on peaceful operations*

Throughout decades of superpower tension during the Cold War, American and Soviet aircrews regularly interacted with one another in an unsung, unusual, and, until now, unknown program called Constant Shotgun.

Department of Defense code names are often created by joining two separate unclassified words that represent the mission. Each "first word" in such a sequence is assigned to a particular service. "Constant" refers to an Air Force program. "Shotgun" was likely chosen to portray the actual activity of sitting in the cockpit with someone else at the controls. What American kid hasn't called out "Shotgun!" to claim the coveted front seat of the family car?

Overseen by Headquarters United States Air Force (HQ USAF), the Federal Aviation Administration (FAA), and the US State Department, our job was to accompany any Soviet aircraft entering United States airspace. We ensured foreign crews understood air traffic control instructions, learned what we could about the people and their aircraft, and prevented them from "accidental" overflight of sensitive ground installations. We were stationed in the cockpit itself as auxiliary crew members during all legs of flight over our sovereign territory.

Though I served for a time as the program's operations

officer, I was the least of all Shotgun pilots. My self-study of the Russian language was wholly insufficient. I had zero experience in crewed aircraft, having spent my entire career in the supersonic T-38 trainer as an instructor and in the U-2 high-altitude reconnaissance single-seat aircraft. Cockpit crew coordination was foreign to me, except for sharing in-flight duties with inexperienced student pilots (who always seemed determined to cause us harm).

All my compadres were so much better equipped: Mike Rodzianko, Frank Peluso, Dick Unser, Al Westrom, Pete Shockey, Chuck Miller, Brian Green (not his real name, nicknamed "Greenie"), and Bill Smith, among others. They were fluent speakers with heavy transport aircraft experience. They pretty much knew what they were doing. The only thing I offered was the enthusiasm of a young, naïve captain who believed he could learn by immersion in a world of Soviet airmen. I also brought good organizational skills to the program, for what that was worth.

I cherish my six-year association with the program. It was one of the best assignments of my forty-year career as an active pilot. As you read, you'll surely agree that my esteemed colleagues and I occupied a unique position as pawns in that much larger drama history has labeled the Cold War.

This anthology contains extraordinary aviation stories experienced during my time among this specialized group of USAF pilots and navigators. It portrays only my singular and myopic view of what transpired and thus is unavoidably incomplete. I recognize that large pieces of the puzzle leading up to each event are missing from my narrative. What I saw is all I can relay.

Dialogue used during the missions is also inexact. I did not record precise conversations in my otherwise well-maintained journal. After forty years, I've had to recreate presumed verbiage to illustrate these honest-to-goodness events. Because of the language barrier, some supposed exchanges may have happened only in my mind. I probably didn't always verbalize my genuine concerns during intense episodes of flight, at least not in a language that the pilot in command could understand. The turmoil expressed through self-talk characterizes the commotion that made all these experiences so memorable.

Please note that several of these stories highlight significant flaws in airmanship among some Soviet (and later Russian) pilots, but I do not intend to denigrate them. I saw many more excellent pilots among our adversary than poor pilots. However, it is those hair-raising moments created by the few hapless aviators that stand out in my mind. By relating them, I share a peculiar piece of unexplored aviation history.

Military pilots, on the whole, are an odd bunch. Though we were trained killers, our "Shotgun" flight experiences brought us all to the stark realization that the "enemy" was like us, and we were like them. As a nation, we should rejoice that the balanced actions of our two governments over the course of forty-two years of restrained conflict allow us to live today in an environment where basement bomb shelters are no longer required and childhood nuclear drills are a practice of the distant past.

And now, please enjoy this record of one man's experience riding Constant Shotgun with the Soviets.

- GLENN R. WHICKER, Colonel, USAF (Retired)
July 2025

Chapter 1 - First Glance

Пе́рвый блин всегда́ ко́мом
"The first pancake is always lumpy"

January 1984

I hung up the telephone, thrilled to the point of whooping across the kitchen.

"Pam," I yelled a little too loudly, "I get to fly with the Soviets!"

My wife of six years understood my dream. The lofty plan coalescing in my head was to eventually become the Air Attaché to the American Embassy in Moscow, USSR.

With cassette tapes, dictionaries, and grammar textbooks at my side, I kept dabbling in the Russian language, however ineffectively, as a step toward securing this goal. However, I was making no progress toward that larger career objective. After three strenuous flights in the T-38 supersonic jet trainer each day, pulling up to 7 G's, sitting through students' bad landings, and briefing and debriefing each flying period ad nauseam, no time remained for other professional pursuits. I'd go home to turn my much-anticipated attention to the beautiful mother of my four-year-old twin girls and their ambitious baby sister. These ladies were my priority.

Although this daily routine of instructing student pilots didn't lend to the crisp concentration necessary to acquire such a difficult dialect, I could fantasize. And a dreamer I was. I attuned my ears to any scuttlebutt that might hint at a language training option within the USAF. Now, years of searching and positioning had finally led me to a portal that could lead to my goal: The 1984 Summer Olympics were coming to Los Angeles.

Why Become a Pilot?

Tech Tab #1

Great question! Not everyone loves flight as much as I do, but I have often wondered why they don't! After four decades of flying, here are my reasons for loving it:

1 – You're never stuck with a single view from your desk. Every minute of every day you fly, you see new breathtaking vistas. It's hard to beat the views on a flight over Zion National Park or the Grand Canyon. Night flight is especially amazing, as the air is generally smooth and clear, you can see for a hundred miles, and the lights of cities mesh with that of the stars.

2 – You recognize the triviality of world problems. From the air, there are no visible borders, no distinction between race or income, no insurmountable barriers such as disease or death. Yes, it's unrealistic to think such things don't exist, but it's also liberating to be free of such concerns, even for a short moment. The "Breakaway Effect" restores faith and hope in humanity.

3 – It is a challenge. Mastering aviation is not easy, nor is it monothematic. (Did I make that word up?) Aviation pulls so many disciplines into a single

enterprise, including aerodynamics, mechanics, meteorology, navigation, teaching, physiology, psychology, health, safety, cartography, communication, organization, research, engineering, performance factors, computation, pilotage, space, human relations, planning, regulation, computers, systematization, hand-eye coordination and vision, to name just a few! No, pilots aren't masters of any of those, but they necessarily study and learn enough about each to become well-rounded, educated generalists.

4 – The rewards are worth it. I'm not a millionaire — I can't even afford my own airplane. Yet, I have seen the world. I have shown it to my family. And all the while, I have provided well for them financially. Retired and with a reasonable income guaranteed for the rest of my life, my wife will be comfortable even after my passing. As my young daughter once said as she watched an aircraft land at Washington's Reagan National Airport:

"Dad, I can't believe they PAY you just to fly airplanes!"
"I can't either, honey, but they do, and I'll take it!"

The Soviet Union, always a strong contender in the Games, was sending a large contingent of athletes and support staff. Because of reciprocity agreements between our governments, all their aircraft would need to be escorted into the US by USAF pilots.

My phone call with Major Michael Rodzianko was brief. As Operations Officer of an obscure program called Constant Shotgun, he needed flight-rated[1] officers who had scored at least a level two on the Russian DLPT.[2] He had pulled my name from a database at the Military Personnel Center (MPC). Would I be available to augment the core Shotgun team for ten days?

Would I ever! I marveled that my minimal speaking ability merited a place on that list, but I wouldn't argue. I was more than excited — I had hit the jackpot!

Or had I? Several months went by with no further communication about the imminent Shotgun flights. All I knew was that a team of two US pilots would meet each incoming Soviet transport aircraft at Alaska's Elmendorf Air Force Base and escort them along the West Coast for landing at L.A. International Airport (LAX). As I passed the time going about my heavy flying duties instructing at Sheppard AFB in Texas, the anticipation of hobnobbing with Soviet crews on their mystifying aircraft was all I could think about.

One evening in mid-May, Pam called me into the family room, where she was watching TV.

"Glenn, have you seen the news? The USSR just announced

---

1. In the Air Force, a "rated officer" is one whose primary job is flying aircraft. In my era, this was generally restricted to pilots and navigators, but today's force has expanded rated opportunities to include combat systems officers, air battle managers, and remotely piloted aircraft (RPA) pilots.
2. Defense Language Proficiency Test

they're refusing to take part in the Olympics. What does that mean for your escort plans?"

In that instant, my high hopes for a first look at the Shotgun mission shattered. Four years earlier, President Jimmy Carter had boycotted the Moscow Olympics in response to the 1979 Soviet invasion of Afghanistan. Now I stood mesmerized as word came that in retaliation, Soviet Premier Konstantin Chernenko was playing the same trick, accusing current President Reagan of spreading "hostile anti-Soviet propaganda."

Tit-for-tat. The harsh reality of global politics was interfering with my personal ambitions.

The only consolation was that my name was at least on someone's radar. My best plan was to dedicate myself to further developing my pilot skills, studying the language, and patiently awaiting the next need for Shotgun escorts.

It took nearly four years for another opening to arise.

If only I was as thin as my patience.

Chapter 2 - Slow Go

Тише едешь, дальше будешь
"Go slower – you will get further"

<u>May 1985</u>

Sixteen months passed. I finished my four-year Texas tour in the supersonic T-38 Talon and was now assigned to the 9th Strategic Reconnaissance Wing at Beale AFB, CA. We added another beautiful baby girl just before the Permanent Change of Station (PCS) to California.

As a First Assignment Instructor Pilot, or FAIP, I had become expert at teaching brand-new Second Lieutenants to fly that demanding but rewarding jet, even though I was barely ahead of them in experience. Recent Undergraduate Pilot

Lt. Glenn Whicker by a T-38 Talon at Sheppard AFB, Texas, in 1981

Training (UPT) graduates make great instructors immediately after earning their wings, and this progression is a widely used practice in the aviation world. It offers young, inexperienced pilots the chance to develop their flying and leadership skills quickly — and subjecting FAIPs to the unwitting hare-brained conspiracies of complete newbies builds character! As they try to plow themselves into the ground through critical in-flight errors, you learn to anticipate their mistakes. Survival depends on your ability to cut them off before they spiral into unrecoverable disasters. Self-preservation is an adept teacher. You either improve rapidly, or you (and the student) die. It's that simple.

I loved the unrivaled T-38 as a training aircraft. Often referred to as "the race car of the Air Force," its symmetrical form, gorgeous aerodynamic lines, lightning speed, and long legs (ability to go extended distances before refueling) inspire. In a word, it was sexy! The intense rush of feeling my body being pushed back into the seat as we smoothly advanced the throttle into full afterburner was undeniable. The beauty of dodging white, puffy clouds, another sleek T-38 scarcely three feet away in fingertip formation, was truly satisfying. Yet I always knew this complex contraption had the potential to harm me if I let my guard down. I was at ease inside its cockpit, but I never allowed myself to become complacent.

T-38 Talon in formation

I first flew with my dad when I was ten. Leading up to that experience, my fascination with airplanes had me spending hours at the Ogden airport, watching "puddle jumpers" come and go. I dreamily wondered how the world would look from up there.

That first flight came in a small Cessna 172 with a mere 120 horsepower engine, less output than a small car built today. We soared from Salt Lake City over the majestic Wasatch and Uinta Mountains to Craig, Colorado, where my parents were part owners of a family ranch. Every summer, my brothers and I would spend a week or two on the farm, hauling hay, driving tractors, and exploring the vast landscape. It was an exciting time, particularly that year, as we opted to fly instead of drive.

I must have linked the aroma of that little Cessna with the stunning views and exhilarating freedom of flying — no roads, stop signs, or traffic cops, just the clear blue sky as a backdrop to some few scattered cotton balls with their billowy tops, and a vantage point previously reserved for only God and fowls.

I get that same intense pleasure today after forty-five years of piloting. Every time I open an aircraft's door or raise a canopy to enter a cockpit, that distinct fragrance hits my nostrils and infuses me with the butterflies of a young man in love. The urge to thoughtfully and gently attend to my paramour pushes away any inkling of fear, distress, or dread.

Can it be just the oil and gas fumes? No, it must be more than that, or it would smell exactly like a car. It doesn't. The unique scent invokes a special transformation that always strikes my psyche, whether I'm approaching a small puddle-jumper aircraft or a powerful military jet for a preflight inspection.

Commercial airliners don't elicit that same sensation. Those large people movers mask true airplane smells, overpowering them with aromas of food, upholstery, luggage, and hordes of human bodies. Passengers on those behemoths never experience the unparalleled tang of raw, turbulent aviating. It's a phenomenal mix of emotions.

First, as you approach the aircraft, your skin comes alive with deep anticipation. The coming thrill envelopes all senses as every cell in your body recalls the joy of skirting across the countryside with a bird's-eye view of a world without borders.

Second, you experience profound respect for the raw energy at your fingertips, a power that man has dreamed of for eternities but harnessed only recently, within my grandfather's lifetime.

Third, you have the immense responsibility of safely piloting an aircraft through the untamed sky, providing an exhilarating encounter with nature, without causing fear or harm to passengers or vehicle.

This is the genuine delight of naked flight, where you must manhandle the yoke in full command, almost as if riding a bucking bronco.

I am convinced a plane's perfume results from the mixture of sweat with gas and oil. It takes little effort to drive a car. In fact, it's easy to let your mind wander far from important duties as you barrel down the highway. But you cannot pilot an aircraft without deep and personal integration with it. Otherwise, the vigorous physics of flight can and will overpower your capacity to maintain control.

The merging of man and machine generates a tangible tension, coordinating aircraft movement with the pilot's will. It is akin to the strain by which a puppeteer manipulates his puppet, yet with much more at stake. Beads of perspiration inevitably result from the concentration required. On approach to landing, you catch yourself automatically wiping unwanted sweat off your hands onto your pant legs and using your shirt sleeve to remove droplets from your forehead. And, like the exchange of a slobbery kiss with the woman you love, the pilot's perspiratory lather absorbs into the plane's seat cushions; it filters through the upholstery and permanently sublimates into the very atmosphere of the cockpit.

Whiffs of this singular concoction of oil, fuel, and passionate sweat combine to produce the power, thrust, and lift that carry us high into the troposphere.

Four years in the sleek T-38 gravity-buster were not enough for me, and I was overjoyed to receive a second assignment in the same plane. It fully satisfied my "need for speed." Other FAIPs in my situation ambitiously looked to transition to a Major Weapon System (MWS), such as a fighter, bomber, or heavy transport; that was the "approved" career progression. However, I had no desire to rush off to a different jet. The steady, unhurried rhythm of an unconventional path suited me just fine. Sticking with the Talon would allow me to be home almost every night with my beautiful wife and four growing daughters. It would also give me more flexibility should Shotgun call again. I felt no urgency to follow the crowd by seeking a more glamorous airplane with a more consequential mission.

At least not yet.

Chapter 3 - The Call

Всякому о́вощу своё вре́мя
"Every vegetable has its time"

17 November 1987, Tuesday

I stood back to admire our shiny '86 Chevrolet Astro van gleaming in the driveway. After two hours of cleaning it inside and out, it had that new car shine again — almost. The very first state-of-the art vehicle we'd ever purchased, I had done a lot of research and negotiating to get just the right deal on wheels for our growing family. It was deep blue, seated eight, and even had rear air-conditioning — the wife's "must-have" option. This beauty cost us a pretty penny, but we intended it to last the rest of our child-rearing days, and we both loved it. After such an enormous investment, I was determined to keep it in pristine condition, complete with regular oil changes, washes, vacuuming, and waxing. My four young daughters tested that ambitious goal by trashing the expensive car every time we went anywhere!

By now, we had lived at Beale AFB in Northern California for two and a half years. I continued flying the sleek supersonic T-38 Talon, but now with more seasoned KC-135, U-2 and SR-71 pilots. My peers challenged me to cross-train into the super-secret high-altitude reconnaissance plane, the U-2.

Learning this new jet was more than difficult. It flew on the edge of space with gobs of sophisticated equipment that provided valuable intelligence to the highest levels of the government.

And it was squirrelly to handle.

Nicknamed the Dragon Lady, when you treated it right, it was like dancing with a lovely lady. But if you mishandled it in the slightest, it transformed it into a fiery dragon, determined to burn you alive!

After becoming fully mission qualified in this Major Weapon System (MWS) on 15 November, I was preparing to embark on my first operational sortie in the U-2 on 7 December, just three weeks hence.

"Glenn, someone from the Pentagon wants to talk to you about … an endless shotgun or something?"

Pam didn't transfer the phrase correctly, so her words were slow to penetrate my otherworldly thoughts. But when they did, the magic word "Shotgun" sent an electric shock straight to the center of my being. My heart ran into the house faster than my feet could carry me to take the call.

Startled and out of breath, I grabbed the telephone and strung the long, coiled cord around the corner into the living room for some undisturbed quiet and buried the old-style phone in my shoulder. Pam quickly hushed our noisy girls and came around to stand by me.

Cupping my hand over the receiver, I whispered, "Pam, did you say the Pentagon? Constant Shotgun? This could be it!"

Then, clearing my throat, I forced my voice to sound confident despite my winded state.

"Hello, this is Glenn. What can I do for you?"

"Hey, Captain Whicker, this is Major Pete Shockey from the Air Force Special Activities Center. Вы говорите по-русски, да? (Vy govorite po-russki, da?)"

Uh-oh, I thought. *He's going to test my very poor Russian!*

"Да, немного (Da, nemnogo)," I managed to blurt out. He had no idea how tiny a "bit" I meant when he asked about my language skills!

"Great!" he continued in English.

Whew! I wiped my brow. That was too easy.

"We're putting together several crews to manage the upcoming Reagan/Gorbachev Nuclear Arms Summit in DC and need every Russian-speaking pilot we can get to escort the half-dozen airplanes supporting the Soviet General Secretary. Would you be available for a special TDY[3] next month from the 8th through the 14th?"

Wow. I felt almost as dizzy as when I had knelt to ask my wife to marry me!

"I'm sure I can!" I replied enthusiastically — though, in the back of my mind, I wondered. Would the squadron release me just as I'd finalized my expensive U-2 training to go off and do something completely unrelated?

We talked for a few more minutes as he got my immediate boss's contact info so he could send an official message requesting my support. Although Lt. Colonel Ash Lafferty wouldn't have the last word on approving me for this special mission, the process needed to start and end with him.

After I hung up the handset, Pam smiled and eagerly asked me to share the news.

"I finally get to fly with the Ruskies!"

When she gets excited, Pam's eyes sparkle. It was one of the special characteristics that drew me in the first time I saw her. Sometimes she dazzled me with a simple, sultry wink. Now she drilled those gorgeous, blazing, and smiling peepers into mine, asking, "When? Where?"

Totally loyal, this girl. We'd been dating only a few months when I first voiced my intent to join the Air Force and become a pilot. A true hometown Utah gal, she knew zilch about military life, yet she immediately supported me, just as she was doing now. "You must make the career decisions," she had told me, but

---

3. Temporary DutY.

she'd be right there with me. How could any man deserve such luck? She was amazing.

We talked. I knew the dates and reason behind the trip, but little more. I had so many questions myself — mostly doubts determined to quash my short-lived high.

"Pam, this might not work. I'm scheduled to go to Korea in two weeks. They're not going to let me disrupt the entire squadron's deployment schedule to send me on a non-related fling!"

The Wing[4] King, as he was known, was a full-bird[5] Colonel who wouldn't understand the significance of this golden opportunity. The U-2 training syllabus had been intense, and now that I was fully trained and at long last useful for our unit's real-world reconnaissance mission, it would be highly unusual to break up my six-month utilization cycle.

U-2 reconnaissance aircraft in flight

Pam tried to calm me. She was prepared to approach the Colonel herself if needed. That's how desperate she was for me to secure the Shotgun gig.

"The brass might worry I'll inadvertently divulge hard-won

---

4. Air Force organizations are, from smallest to largest, a flight, squadron, group and wing. The wing commander, usually at least a full colonel, carries a lot of weight in both authority and responsibility.
5. A full colonel, as opposed to a lieutenant or "light" colonel, wears an eagle rank insignia; thus the nickname, "full-bird."

details of the magic formula that allows us to fly so high," I whined. The USSR had never duplicated the U-2's extreme altitude, and they actively pursued inside information, hoping to attain to the levels of performance the Lady had since 1955. By the 1990s, their Mystic aircraft would almost match it, but even then they only produced two of its kind and those never produced any strategic value.

"You're no aerospace genius," Pam brought me down to reality. "How could they possibly get anything out of a dummy like you!" She laughed, making me smile. After all, I was just a high-flying bus driver! I knew nothing of value related to design or engineering.

"But will my Russian language skills be enough?" I worried. After only one measly semester of Russian in college years before, I could barely write the cryptic Cyrillic alphabet and read a few basic words.

Pam was having none of my doubts and pessimism. "Your Russian proficiency might be totally inadequate, but you somehow scored high enough to get the language listed on your official records. That seems to be all they're looking for! They wouldn't have called you if they didn't think you could do the job." And with that, she put a lid on the downward spiral of my mood for the moment.

However, I still had ample time to worry about the plan not coming together.

23 November 1987, Monday

Three full workdays and a weekend had passed since the official request from Washington had reached the Wing King's desk, and I still hadn't heard his decision. The wait was excruciating. 24 November was the last day before Thanksgiving break, and I had to inform the Shotgun people by that afternoon about my availability for escorting the Soviet flights. They had to have time to put two-person teams together, draw up orders, gather passports, and apply for visas, as well as book tickets to the various points of embarkation.

Finally, Lafferty called me into the squadron office.

"Whick," he said in a dejected tone. My neck and shoulder muscles tensed in anticipation. Lafferty was a good-natured guy who always ventured to give his pilots the best working environment possible. To have him start a conversation with that negative inflection didn't bode well.

"You're asking a lot here, you know. We get you to the point of being useful to our Peacetime Aerial Reconnaissance Program (PARPRO[6]), and you want to go gallivanting off to fly *with* the enemy instead of *against* it?"

I knew I'd put everyone in a tough situation.

"Yes, Sir," I replied, respectful of the difficult position he occupied. I wasn't inclined to give up the argument yet. "Even though the U-2 is considered an essential national asset, these Shotgun flights are helping bring about huge advancements in nuclear arms control. Would Captain Feda be able to swap timelines with me — he's ready and rarin' to go TDY to Korea."

"Well," he continued. "The Wing King wasn't easy to convince ..."

"... but, we just approved your dadgum Constant Shotgun trip. You're lucky the request came from the State Department; they somehow managed to trump even Strategic Air Command (SAC) headquarters. Hope you enjoy it. Now, get out of here!" he smiled. He was a friendly dude, but no mincer of words. I'm

---

6. For a short, fascinating history of the origins of PARPRO, see https://tinyurl.com/ColdWarRecon

sure he could see my broad smile through the back of my head as I shut his door behind me.

SAC HQ? I didn't realize the request for support had traveled that far up the chain of command, to a 4-Star General, no less. No wonder it took almost an entire week!

Pam smiled coyly at the good news.

I immediately called Major Shockey at AFSAC in Virginia. Little did I know that quiet afternoons obsessing over my new van were gone. I was about to embark on the adventure of a lifetime. My time had come.

"I'm cleared hot," I told Shockey. "So, what's the plan?"

Chapter 4 - Gander

Красиво жить не запретишь
"You cannot forbid living beautifully"

1 December 1987, Tuesday

As I finished packing for my first ten-day Soviet trip, I must have been talking a blue streak, and the entire family could feel my excitement. Pilots often refer to going all out as "balls-to-the-wall,"[7] a reference to pushing the throttle all the way to the firewall. That was definitely my attitude with this potential assignment.

"You realize," I said to Pam as I neatly folded my flight suit into the suitcase, "if I get really good at this Shotgun gig, I may snag an air attaché job in Moscow someday."

She shrugged. "You never know!" Pam trusted I'd always take care of her and the kids, and perhaps she fostered some enjoyment from the bright enthusiasm I consistently showed as I developed my career.

Looking back, I realize I should have had a bit more of a listening ear during those younger days and taken her wishes and feelings more into consideration. Her heart wasn't in what I was suggesting. She had no desire to live behind the Iron Curtain

---

7. In many planes, several flight controls are actuated by a ball-shaped handle. A throttle, for example, must be pushed fully forward, to the firewall (the panel that separates the engine compartment from the cockpit) in order to produce full power. The stick, or yoke, is also pushed to the firewall to initiate a high-speed dive. Thus, pushing the "balls" to the (fire)wall figuratively means doing something with gusto, using maximum effort. It is the aviation equivalent of "putting the pedal to the metal."

with four little children. She'd been around the block a time or two and knew living conditions would be bleak if we were to get that kind of assignment, but she let me flounder in my wildest dreams.

I had a dream and a plan, and I was determined to make it work while simultaneously cherishing my family. I was consumed with my hopes.

And Pam loved me nonetheless.

2 December 1987, Wednesday

Constant Shotgun rules required American pilots to catch inbound Soviet flights on their last stop before entering US airspace. Today, that meant Gander, Newfoundland, Canada. But my itinerary confused[8] me. Air Canada was on strike, so all Canadian Pacific flights were full as they graciously accommodated passengers bumped from their competitor. SATO (Scheduled Airline Traffic Offices), the civilian travel contractor used by the Air Force, found a commuter flight from Saint John, New Brunswick, to Halifax, Nova Scotia, and then on to Gander. When I looked at the map, I mistook St. John's, which is close to my destination in Newfoundland, for Saint John, New Brunswick. I couldn't understand why they had me backtracking! I guess good 'ol John the Apostle was popular in Canada — every province seemed to name a town after him!

Every Shotgunner fell in love with the beauty of Gander, which lay on the northeastern quadrant of Newfoundland, the

---

8. Another point of confusion didn't help. The clock in Gander is offset a half-hour from the rest of the world! When it's 10:30 a.m. in Boston, it's 12:00 noon in Gander. It makes time conversion a bit harder than it needs to be.

world's sixteenth largest island. Over the years, I returned there often as my association with the program expanded.

On the flight from Saint John, I sat next to Mr. Rupert Short, a school principal in Lewisporte. He seemed nervous about flying, so I tried to ease his mind by telling him I was a USAF pilot.

"If these guys can't handle things, I'll get you down safely," I added jokingly.

"Why's an American officer going to Gander, eh?" he politely wondered out loud.

"We're escorting some Russian planes to Washington for a big summit."

"Eh, what a game!" he said, possibly thinking that a nuclear arms treaty was a long shot.

"I'm hopeful," I replied. "This Gorbachev fellow is a whole new kind of animal. He seems to be breaking the mold of the old Soviet oligarchy."

We had a very congenial conversation for the rest of the flight, and he schooled me in the uniqueness of the Gander airport. "In the '30s," he said, "ours was the largest in the world, with four runways."

Gander, Newfoundland, is strategically located on the east coast of Canada and is often called the "Crossroads of the World." During WW II, its location made it the ideal refueling point for aircraft crossing the Atlantic en route to Europe, and some 20,000 Allied fighter jets and bombers took off from this cozy little town to engage in big European battles.

Post-war commercial aviation also loved Gander as the perfect halfway point between Europe and Florida or Houston, and it soon developed into the ideal refueling spot. To encourage this, the town built a modern, friendly, and efficient international airport, complete with customs services and duty-free shops. Thus, when Shotgun missions proliferated in the late 1980s, it became the most common meeting point for relatively short-legged aircraft such as the IL-76. Flights arriving from across the North Atlantic or returning from the CONUS[9] frequented Gander; we all loved the invigorating and hospitable environment.

Rupert continued. "By the '80s, Communist countries started using Gander's superb facilities for flights between Cuba and Russia, Poland, Czechoslovakia, and East Germany. Then passengers began to realize that stopovers here offered the perfect opportunity to deplane and declare political asylum. You wouldn't believe how many Eastern Bloc citizens jumped ship here."

Customs and immigration policies had to be tightened, so developers specifically built facilities with a conveniently split terminal to keep North American travelers separated from foreign tourists and visitors. The modern terminal was divided into two very controlled sectors: the international side and the domestic side. Foreign travelers were required to remain within the international section, where there was no sanctuary possible.

"Yeah," I jumped in. "The whole reason we have to escort these summit flights is because Aeroflot was banned from US skies back in 1983 after the Soviets shot down Korean Air Lines Flight 007."[10]

Mr. Short enjoyed our interchange, and he generously offered me a ride from the airport to a local bed and breakfast.

---

9. CONtinental United States (the lower 48).
10. President Ronald Reagan revoked Aeroflot's license to operate flights into and out of the US until 2 August 1990.

3 December 1987, Thursday

Though we couldn't have known it then, Gander would become even more famous in 2001 for its tremendous hospitality to the thousands of airline passengers from ninety-three different countries who got stuck there on September 11. After terrorists flew airliners into the Twin Towers in New York City, the Pentagon, and the Pennsylvania countryside, killing 2,977 people and injuring over six thousand others, authorities implemented a never-before-used contingency plan in the skies over America, a procedure code-named "SCATANA."[11] SCATANA prohibited any aircraft from entering our airspace and grounded almost all planes inside the United States. They forced over four thousand airplanes out of the air within a few hours. Inbound flights already airborne from Europe needed a safe place to land before reaching our closed borders, and the City of Gander[12] welcomed those 6,700 diverted air travelers with warm, open arms.

The Cape Cod Inn where Mr. Short took me was pleasant and oozing with geniality. A lovely middle-aged woman named Marg ran it. The Royal Canadian Air Force had assigned her husband to 9 Wing Gander, which is based alongside the international airport. It wasn't unusual to run across uniformed Canadian military personnel throughout town.

"Cozy" doesn't begin to describe this golden B&B. Marg's attitude in providing such a hospitable repose was captured during an interview with the LA Times in 1991: "Oh, it's a dangerous world out there today, isn't it? But Newfoundland is

---

11. Security Control of Air Traffic and Air Navigation Aids.
12. For a fascinating treatise on this remarkable little town's unsurpassed hospitality during that crisis, see https://tinyurl.com/Gander9-11

as peaceful as ever. Yes, yes, yes, it is."[13]

Shotgun pilots slept on soft queen-size beds covered with down duvets in private bedrooms upstairs. We had full use of their front room, which had a large cable TV, a warm fireplace, and a well-equipped kitchen outfitted with complimentary hot chocolate, sodas, and snacks. Marg provided us with steaming and sumptuous meals. The washer and dryer were available free of charge, and we could make both personal and official calls on their old-style rotary telephone, patched through to the nearby base operator. It was almost like we were part of Marg's family!

You can be sure we treated her well. We felt very blessed to have found their little business. After a night at the Cape Cod, we were refreshed and ready to handle our important in-flight duties. We frequently hung out there quite comfortably while patiently waiting for a Soviet transport that failed to materialize until days after it was scheduled to do so.

Major Shockey insisted that all Shotgun pilots be in place early for this highly visible mission so that we could familiarize ourselves with each other, explore the facilities at the airport, and receive a thorough briefing on the upcoming events.

Newfoundland is breathtakingly beautiful. During descent from cruise altitude, the fragrant smell of pine emanates from immense forests across the island. Its cleansing freshness wafts in through the cockpit air vents. Long before breaking out of the clouds, you know you're in pristine country, and the frequent rain only intensifies the luscious aroma.

But we were there for serious business. The planned Shotgun trips this round were connected to the historic Reagan / Gorbachev Summit in Washington, DC, scheduled for December 8-10. Ten USAF-rated linguists were needed to man the five

---

13. https://tinyurl.com/GanderBeauty

Soviet aircraft supporting Mikhail Gorbachev's entourage. Three IL-62 Classic passenger jets would carry the Soviet VIPs and their team from RAF[14] Brize-Norton in England directly to Andrews AFB in Maryland. One cargo-laden IL-76 Candid was to stop in Gander on its way to drop off the Premier's armored ZiL limousine at Andrews. Rather than park there for several days, that aircraft would immediately return to the USSR. In addition, they routed a second, empty IL-76 through Gander. This was my assigned aircraft, with Sam Blanchard as my partner. We were to deadhead (fly with no cargo aboard) to Havana and wait, poised to pick up the Soviet leader's communications equipment and his armored limo after the summit concluded. Though I can't be sure, I believe it was the Soviets' own decision not to park overnight on US soil. I never saw any correspondence from our side prohibiting them from parking there for a few days, but it all worked out to my advantage — I got a free trip to Cuba!

I initially wondered why the popular General Secretary needed to transport his own vehicle halfway around the world to ride the mere fifteen miles from Andrews AFB to the White House via Suitland Parkway. It later dawned on me that, considering the state of world affairs, he could not, or would not, trust Americans to provide him with adequate protection while visiting. Such political cat-and-mouse games were constant between the world's two superpowers.

Little did Gorbachev know the superstar status he would achieve here in the States. He and his lovely wife Raisa represented a beacon of hope that the Cold War could finally die without coming to military blows. Instead of facing a hostile enemy during their visit, the Gorbachev's experienced a level of adoration seldom achieved by even our own US presidents.

---

14. Royal Air Force of the United Kingdom.

Chapter 5 - Song of Peace

Мир да лад -- большой клад
"Peace and harmony is great treasure"

8 December 1987, Tuesday

The big day was just hours away, and I was extremely excited! After a decade of linguistic study, preparation, career positioning, and a canceled opportunity almost four years before, I would finally have the chance to rub shoulders with Soviet aviators and fly in a Russian-made aircraft! This particular trip had an even greater punch to it—we were flying to Havana, Cuba, the only Communist country in our hemisphere.

From my high school history classes, I knew that President John F. Kennedy had prohibited American travel there since Fidel Castro took power in the early 1960s. Those restrictions were still in place by 1987, so I was delighted to visit where few in the US had been in the last quarter century. This was going to be an experience practically like traveling behind the Iron Curtain, a journey I longed for and hoped that Shotgun would eventually offer me.

Having lived in Argentina from 1974 to 1976 as a missionary, I spoke Spanish a thousand times better than I spoke Russian. I already loved and respected one Latin American culture and, with a scheduled two-day layover in Cuba, was eager to be exposed to another. The ol' *yearn-to-learn* juices flowed, and it was a great feeling.

This is what has always made life so interesting to me — the thrill of new knowledge and experiences. Boredom has no place with excitement like this lying ahead.

Early in the day, I watched General Secretary Mikhail

Gorbachev and President Ronald Reagan sign the Intermediate-Range Nuclear Forces Treaty (INF) on TV. It was emotional. By eliminating an entire category of atomic weapons in one flourish of the pen, they drastically reduced the risk of war, increasing security in the European arena.[15] It was meaningful to be part of this historic event in some small way.

During my childhood and early adult years, the big, mysterious, super-powerful Soviet "Bear" was out there to eat us. As schoolchildren, we often crouched under flimsy desks during timed drills to "protect" ourselves from nuclear attack. Enterprising businesses profited from selling bomb shelters to nervous homeowners. The US military maintained a presence around the world, ready to retaliate with over 30,000 warheads at a moment's notice. These missiles could travel up to twenty-three times faster than the speed of sound through space, potentially annihilating the Soviet menace before impact.

Our nuclear Triad[16] ensured a "measured" response to any dynamic threat. Plugged in and primed, we were always ready to react should the enemy launch any of his copious and nefarious wares. Thankfully, both the USSR and the US proved to be rational actors, and the conflict between us never became hot. Though tense and often uncomfortable,[17] there was a sustained "holding back" of lethal animosity, avoiding the certain devastation that would have destroyed life as we knew it. The

---

15. https://tinyurl.com/1987INFtreaty
16. The three delivery methods available to the US to deliver nuclear weapons: strategic bombers (air), inter-continental ballistic missiles (land) and missile-firing submarines (sea). All three legs of the Triad are controlled by US Strategic Command in Omaha, NE.
17. For a historical reference on just how dicey things got at times, reference the U-2 Incident (1960), the Bay of Pigs invasion (1961), and the Cuban Missile Crisis (1962).

determined actions of the world's most powerful leaders reduced a significant part of the peril. The Cold War was cooling. It was the right thing to do.

Sam, my partner on this first excursion, was also new to Constant Shotgun. He had one mission under his belt. Just last week, he'd proven his Russian was no better than mine as he made his maiden trip as an escort. Thankfully, we knew the aircraft's radio operator had at least enough proficiency in "*Angliyskiy*" to perform the required communication duties. He would help us out. English, after all, is the universal language of aviation.

9 December 1987, Wednesday

We met the IL-76 crew at the airport. I was nervous, not knowing what to expect, but I projected confidence as I greeted the Soviet airmen in their spiffy military uniforms, shaking their hands firmly and trying out my juvenile Russian on them. Despite their heavy preflight tasks, they treated us well and seemed happy to welcome us aboard.

As we entered the aircraft, I was stunned that each of them immediately changed from their uniforms into jogging attire. It looked much cozier, but it wasn't something I'd seen done by any other airline. My father flew cargo airlines for over forty years, and he always had to wear the prescribed formal attire of a coat and tie. Shotgunners wore civilian clothing rather than uniforms while traveling commercially to and from our points of embarkation, mainly to downplay our military affiliation. I learned it was customary for us, too, to change into something more comfortable once aboard the Soviet carriers. So Sam and I followed their example and donned our familiar and cushy green Nomex flight suits.

The airplane had a very noticeable smell to it, different from what I was used to, and somewhat unpleasant. The normal mixture of fuel, hydraulics, and oil had somehow combined with a barrage of stockyard and unusual food smells. Mixed in was the aroma of strong black rye bread and the sweet scent of a type of blackberry jam they ate. They called it *varenye*. Over time, I learned to expect that very distinct tang in all their cargo airplanes.

They gave us free rein to walk around the plane and get a feel for it. It seemed like a normal bare-bones cargo airlifter at first glance, but I quickly discovered some obvious and quite interesting differences. The altimeter displayed height using meters rather than feet, they adjusted the barometric pressure to millibars in place of inches, and airspeed was measured in kilometers per hour instead of knots. I had to have my nifty little "whiz wheel"[18] handy to make quick conversions to more familiar measurements.

However, the dual-level cockpit was the most unique characteristic of the airplane. The two pilots, radio operator, and flight engineer all manned duty stations in the upper level, while the navigator scored the best seat in the house. Directly beneath the pilots, the lower deck sported a broad, panoramic view through ceiling-to-floor glass windows. It created a sense of suspension in mid-air and was beyond breathtaking!

Handheld circular slide rule, the E6B "whiz wheel"

---

18. Basically, the E6B flight computer was a circular slide rule used by pilots in an era before electronic flight calculators became common.

The route of flight from Gander to Havana was a long leg of 2,040 nautical miles on an average course of 248°. At 430 knots cruise speed, the no-wind time en route would be about five hours and thirty minutes.

For the entire first half of the trip, my partner and I would have no real duties because we weren't flying directly inside the US. We wouldn't even be landing inside the US on this trip. We would be in American-owned skies for most of the way, though, sliding along the Eastern Seaboard to Cuba's José Martí Airport. According to international law, all airspace within twelve nautical miles of the coastal boundary of a sovereign nation belongs to that country. In case of an in-flight emergency, our only option would be to divert to a Stateside airport, in which case our services would be very useful.

Our paper TDY orders were the most unusually wide-open I'd ever seen. They were called "blanket" orders because they were indeed like a blank check! Changes to airline tickets? No problem! We could go to and from and in and between anywhere we needed to accomplish the mission. Fund cites authorized the use of rental cars and hotels without regard to cost. This kind of flexibility was necessary because of the fluid circumstances surrounding Shotgun's commission, but it was still amazing to be allowed such freedom of movement after having spent over a decade traveling on regular, stringent orders.

Cargo planes aren't generally soundproof like commercial airliners. The steady roar of engines and airflow around the fuselage are constant and loud. My aviator dad taught me the importance of safeguarding my hearing by always wearing earplugs. Such precaution was emphasized by the Air Force when I entered the flying industry. My father knew too many old pilots who had gone deaf early, and he intended to proactively protect that precious sense. None of the Soviets wore any ear protection at all. I found that odd.

They also kept the aircraft uncomfortably warm in flight. It not only caused dehydration but made me sleepy when I wasn't engaged in one of our responsibilities. Before entering our airspace, I fell asleep in the cargo bay for fifteen to twenty minutes.

I was wearing my expandable earplugs to protect my hearing, so I was a bit surprised to wake up and hear a distinct, beautiful melody.

I looked around to see where the music was coming from. *There must be some fantastic stereo system in this baby*, I thought to myself. The sound was orchestral in quality and very alluring!

As it continued, I began to recognize the tune. It was a church hymn titled "Come, Follow Me."[19]

Wait a minute; seven Soviet crew members are on this plane. Their entire country is atheist. Why would any of them play a song with Christian themes? It perplexed me.

Turns out, there was no stereo. Yet the power of that song continued to invade my senses for several minutes, clear and full. I sat still and reveled in the beauty of it, the words of each verse flowing through my head, for I knew them by heart:

"For thus alone can we be *one*, with God's own loved, Begotten Son."

Ok, Lord. I get the message. Here were two Americans being hurled through the skies in a so-called "enemy" aircraft. Every textbook I'd ever read and all my military training said these guys were not to be trusted. My country placed us on board specifically because of that fact; our job was to ensure they didn't try any funny stuff like veering off course to overfly a sensitive

---

19. ChurchofJesusChrist.org/music/library/hymns/come-follow-me (emphasis added)

area. But despite that mistrust, we were working together to support the common goal of elevating world peace. The two most powerful leaders in the world were right now meeting in a brave effort to wind down the long-lived tensions between us by removing deadly nuclear firepower from each side.

Our two nations were coming together in unity, just as those lyrics directed.

I glanced around at these foreigners, and a new emotion washed over me all at once: these were my brothers. We even looked like relatives. If you could extract any of us and plop us in a neutral setting, give us identical clothing and matching haircuts, expel bits of lingering odors, and prevent verbal speech, no one in the world could distinguish an American from a Russian. All that was keeping us from the brotherhood intended by God were errant man-made philosophies.

"Time to head to the cockpit," Sam said.

We were soon to hit the intersection in the sky named DAVES, directly east of Pease AFB, New Hampshire (now Portsmouth International Airport). It was our moment to get upstairs to monitor our routing and radio communications as we entered US territory. We jumped into action.

Chapter 6 - The Candid

Видна́ пти́ца по полёту
"The bird is known by its flight"

9 December 1987, Wednesday (continued)

With our Mickey-Mouse-ear headsets donned, Sam and I took our appointed places and listened to the radio and intercom chatter to confirm that we maintained the approved routing. Sam went to the upper cabin with the pilots, engineer, and radio operator, while I stayed below with the navigator, Aleksei. He was the one I worked with most closely to ensure these foreign flyboys flew the approved route.

The glass-bottomed floor featured in the nose of the IL-76, NATO[20] codename Candid, fascinated me. The magnificent view at our feet was thrilling, with the entire forward portion of the

Navigator station on lower deck of IL-76 1

---

20. North Atlantic Treaty Organization.

floor composed of nothing but windows. When skies are clear, the nav can see the ground directly below the flight path and confirm the aircraft's location by referencing landmarks. It's kinda heady — sitting as far forward as possible, the sensation is similar to Leonardo or Kate standing with arms spread wide on the bow of the Titanic.

I just had to ask.

"*Pochemu u vas zdes' tak mnogo okon?*" Why did they build the plane with all these windows?

Aleksei, the best English speaker on the Soviet crew, answered in English. "We do not have so many VORs[21] in Soviet Union; I must see the ground to navigate."

That answer didn't sit square with me. Since clouds cover almost seventy percent of the Earth at any moment, professional pilots will necessarily spend a lot of flight time without outside references. Sure, we also practiced visual navigation in every airplane I'd ever flown, but none had windows like this! The closest we got was the U-2 spy plane, which had what we called "the upside-down periscope," a little glass bubble protruding from the underside of the plane through which one could see straight below. A series of mirrors transferred the image to the viewsight in the cockpit. Through that window's small aperture, the entire world underneath the plane opened up into a six-inch prism right in front of the pilot's face. It was handy at times, but only a peephole compared to the vastness of the IL-76's glass floor.

I later realized this was not merely a transport aircraft. Its other military functions included air drops (flinging supplies out of the back end to support ground troops) and releasing

---

21. VHF Omnidirectional Range stations are ground-based navigation radio aids.

paratroopers over a target. In the past, these crews also trained for bombing missions and aerial firefighting. The broad visibility provided by the windows would certainly be advantageous to such efforts.

We ate well. The crew had been kind enough to arrange for a catered box lunch for Sam and me from the Canadians before we left, though they themselves consumed their usual potato soup fare. I tasted their black bread, which had a strong rye flavor, and their jam. They also shared a drink concentrate made from cranberries that just needed hot water. All of it was surprisingly delicious!

When time allowed, I moseyed around the aircraft, itching to satisfy my curiosity. The loadmaster sat alone in the back cargo bay reading *Pravda*, the Soviet newspaper purporting "Truth." I noticed it was only six pages long. His eyes widened in astonishment as he beheld the immense thickness of the day's New York Times I pulled out of my bag.

"We don't have time to sit around and read so much," he said. "In Russia, they only put important news in the paper." Still, he wanted to take a peek at ours. As he thumbed through it, he stopped at the movie section, which consisted of ten full pages.

"Is that all you do, is watch movies?"

I should have answered, "Yeah, when we're not reading newspapers!"

The sky intersection named DAVES (coordinates N42°56.74' W67°30.45' along Jet Route J585; exactly 150 miles outside the US mainland from Nantucket, Rhode Island) marked our first reporting point. Shotgun crews were required to get on the high frequency (HF) radio to call Headquarters USAF at the Pentagon with an "Ops Normal" broadcast. HF was the only type of radio that could traverse the distance to the Pentagon by bouncing its waves off the ionosphere, and the transmission gave those in authority a heads-up that our mission was proceeding smoothly. It also allowed us to update our ETA. The Pentagon relayed those position reports to the USAF Special Activities Center, our point of contact at FAA International, and the US Department of State, which ultimately oversaw these missions.

After exchanging radio pleasantries, our focus shifted to ensuring that the Soviets understood and followed all Air Traffic Control instructions. If the crew didn't fully catch a radio call, we stepped in to interpret or notify controllers we needed further clarification. Most often, there was no problem, though sometimes the incredibly busy East Coast controllers spoke at such a breakneck speed that even I had trouble keeping up with them!

Staying on course was also of the highest importance. FAA International provided us with specific flight paths. We were not to deviate from them except in an emergency or under other unusual circumstances. This had a specific purpose: to prevent our superpower rival from overflying restricted areas such as nuclear power plants, government facilities, or top-secret testing grounds. The air traffic controllers weren't always aware of those parameters, however, and it was the Shotgunners' job to let ATC know if we couldn't accept a requested modification to our flight plan.

Another important aspect of our in-flight tasks that might seem obvious to the reader, but of which we pretended to be indifferent, was the standard cloak-and-dagger game played by every country from the beginning of time. Everyone did it, but no one admitted to it. We were gleaning as much information as possible about this alien airplane, its occupants' lives and political views, and any cargo it carried. In short, we were trying to expand US understanding of our sworn enemy.

So I openly carried a camera, and nobody shot me. I was very obvious about it, and although I took some flak from one person on board, none of the actual flight crew had any problem with my snoopiness. At least, they said nothing and I'm still alive. Perhaps they only pretended not to be interested as well. Who knows? They were excited to see the United States and even showed some eagerness to tell me about their plane, their people, and their country. That seems to be a consistent generality about humans; they like to talk about themselves.

And I was all ears.

When not steeped in my in-flight obligations, I took many pictures from both the up- and downstairs cockpits, as well as the cargo compartment. I got a few good shots of the exterior while on the ground and photos of several crew members. Unfortunately, few of my photos turned out, and even fewer survived the decades of moving households every three years with the Air Force.

A well-dressed man sat in the back, apart from the other passengers and quiet as a mouse. He didn't speak to me, or apparently to anyone, but I caught him looking my way several times with what seemed to be a sort of wariness.

"Who's the dude in the sharp Armani suit sitting down there in the cargo bay?" I asked Aleksei.

"Oh, he's just the political officer."

"Political officer?" I parroted.

"You know what a political officer is, don't you?"

Not exceptionally savvy as to the Communist way of life in 1987, I expressed my naïveté by answering that I did not.

Aleksei whispered, "He's the KGB plant to make sure none of us defect during our trip across the USA." Then he winked.

Wow, I thought. Could it be that this adversary's superpower status was just a façade masking their sense of inferiority?

Almost every one of my early Shotgun flights would have an

assigned KGB political officer. Of course, it wasn't always the same guy, but since none of them ever introduced themselves by name, I'll refer to them collectively as "Graysuit" throughout this book.

I'll never fully understand the subtleties of the relationship between those KGB officers and the rest of the aircrew. They had no flight duties. Their sole purpose, as far as I knew, was to prevent crew members from seeking asylum while in the United States, though I know at least one such defection took place during a Shotgun trip.

These spooks weren't too fond of Americans on their aircraft and always kept a close eye on us. When I wandered around to photograph more of the aircraft, this Graysuit decided he needed to intervene. Without expressly forbidding photography (he didn't have the authority to do so), he offered a reason why I shouldn't.

"Is bad luck take pictures while flight," he said in very broken English. "Make bad landing."

Never mind that a couple of his own countrymen were snap-happy, capturing images of us Americans with them as we flew along. (Selfies existed long before that term was coined.)

As we approached Cuba, I was bursting with anticipation.

What was a Communist country like?

Was the relationship between Soviets and Cubans cordial, reciprocal, or just tolerant?

Did the locals view the USSR as an occupier or a savior?

Did Cubans appreciate their own government or despise it?

How aware were they of the promises and potential America offered?

I would soon discover some surprising answers.

Chapter 7 - José Martí

Копейка рубль бережёт
"A kopeck saves a ruble"

9 December 1987, Wednesday (continued)

Despite Graysuit's warnings, once we left US airspace and set up for the approach to José Martí International Airport in Havana, I positioned myself in the lower cockpit to capture more pictures and get an up-close aerial view of this mysterious Caribbean island nation.

What a beautiful sight it was! There were miles and miles of beaches, a plethora of differently-hued vegetation, rolling hills, and even mountains—a true tropical paradise. I could see why it was such a popular destination before Kennedy's travel prohibition.

Excited to witness a landing from a glass-bottom boat, I sat mesmerized as the earth got closer and closer to my feet (and face). Ground rush is a phenomenon they warned us about in pilot training. When recovering from a stall, you can get overwhelmed by the speed at which the ground is approaching, panic, and instinctively pull back harder on the stick than you should, deepening the stall and effectively sealing your fate. Instead, one should actually push forward on the yoke to regain flying airspeed and then gently increase back pressure to pull out of the fall. It's counterintuitive and difficult to implement because your brain rebels against increasing the already uncomfortable descent rate, even momentarily.

Sitting at the bottom of the nose of the glassy IL-76 lower cockpit gave a whole new meaning to that up-to-now purely academic term, "ground rush." As we settled onto the runway, I caught myself raising my feet off the floor to make sure I wouldn't slam into the ground, hoping fretfully that the pilot was going to flare in time to save my bacon. The sensation was similar to the overwhelming need to duck when you walk beneath helicopter blades, even though you logically know the blades are whirling several feet above you.

From my perspective, the landing flare didn't come quickly enough. I honestly thought we were going to become a splattered mess of bones, tissue, and blood. Thankfully, the pilot knew what he was doing and arrested the aircraft's descent at what seemed the very last second. As we touched down smoothly onto the tarmac, my tensed muscles relaxed in gratitude. I'd survived my first landing in a Soviet aircraft.

Almost immediately after touchdown, I was in for another surprise. Kerplunk-plunk!

"What was that?" I asked Aleksei, perplexed. It sounded like a tire had blown or we had hit an animal.

"We just crossed the tracks," he answered.

"Tracks? What do you mean tracks?" I said.

"This airport has a railroad that crosses the main runway."

"You've got to be kidding me! Why would anyone ever put rails across a runway, let alone at a highly trafficked international airport?"

Aleksei shrugged. To him, it didn't seem so strange, but I couldn't believe it. How could airport planners consider blending a jet runway with a railway—the two plainly don't mix! Which monstrous steel contraption would win if an airliner bounding down the runway at 100+ mph played chicken with a locomotive?

This odd combination also surprised my boss when he flew into Cuba to pick up supplies for the Armenian earthquake relief effort a couple of years later. Colonel Westrom's words:

"We were approaching José Martí Airport after dark and the runway lights were visible from quite a distance. I was a tad confused by what appeared to be an amber rotating beacon about halfway down the airfield on the right. It wasn't until we crossed midfield on the runway that I realized that the beacon was on a train, holding for us at the side of the runway! There was a definite ka-thump as we passed over the tracks at about sixty knots."[22]

Other odd things also struck me as we rolled off onto the taxiway. I noticed haphazard, above-ground wiring connecting the runway edge lights. Besides the natural weather damage inherent in exposed electrical wiring, what about exposure to lawnmowers, rodents, or even opportunistic vandals? Water, sun, and wind would easily accelerate the deterioration of this essential lighting for nighttime operations.

I also saw a constant stream of trash whisking across the runway. FOD, or Foreign Object Damage, can be a major detriment to jet engines, tires, and other costly aircraft components. Most airports have active programs to minimize FOD. I'd never seen so much of it anywhere else.

But my greatest surprise didn't occur until after shutdown. As we deplaned, I noticed that as the engineer was doing his routine post-flight inspection, he would carefully smash what appeared to be a glob of red chewing gum onto the metal closure of the engine cowling. He would then use an antique seal matrix or die to push a unique impression into the ball of wax he had just stuck in place. He repeated this task on each of the four engines.

I asked why. *"Zachem ty eto delayesh'?"*

"We cannot trust Cubans," he said. "In past, they sabotage

---

22. I later discovered that flagmen protected the crossing on each side of the runway, and by 1992, the railway had been rerouted to the west.

engines while we away. Put sugar into gas lines."

"So these wax seals alert you if the engines have been tampered with?"

"*Tochno!* First thing I look in preflight. If seal is broken, I look deep before we fly again."

Wow. There it was. The Big Soviet Bear did not think highly of their little Cuban cousins.

As I walked with the crew into the terminal to do paperwork and eventually head to the hotel, my mind raced. Why would Cubans try such nasty stunts on their supposed benefactors? It was my impression the Soviet Union supplied much of the money that built the infrastructure on the island.

I soon found out the mistrust was mutual.

Years later, I came to the realization that the deep suspicion ingrained into the aircrew possibly had its roots in our own American history. More than twenty-five years before this trip, in 1959, the Soviet–Cuban honeymoon began. Two years later, JFK rose to the US presidency. He was intent on stifling communist influence in the Western Hemisphere, and his administration was especially concerned with Fidel Castro's Cuba, which was a mere ninety nautical miles from US territory at its closest point. Even after the Bay of Pigs debacle,[23] Kennedy continued to support CIA efforts to upend Castro's government. One method of subduing and undermining Fidel was by "infiltrating small groups of fifteen to twenty men each into various points of the country" to perform "acts of terrorism, various [acts] of subversion, acts of sabotage, etc."[24]

Though I've never been able to uncover documented

---

23. *The Brilliant Disaster: JFK, Castro and America's Doomed Invasion of Cuba's Bay of Pigs* by Jim Rasenberger.
24. https://tinyurl.com/BayOfPigsDebacle

evidence of such an act of sabotage on a Soviet aircraft, it seems likely to me that such incidents occurred, leading Soviet aircrews to be constantly on the lookout for disruptive behavior in and around Cuban airfields.

Chapter 8 - La Habana

Кто не рискует, тот не пьет шампанского
"Who does not take risks, does not win"

10 December 1987, Thursday

My journey to then-forbidden Cuba included a two-night vacation-like stay where we bunked in a sketchy hotel known as El Tritón. I will never forget the name or the experience of staying under the protection of a gigantic statue with his trident perched at the ready. "El Tritón" translates to "Merman," or "God of the Sea," the son of Poseidon. Today, the hotel goes by the name "Neptuno-Tritón" and continues to receive the same horrible reviews I gave it almost forty years ago. The management there just doesn't understand the concept of cleanliness or customer service.

We had a full day to ourselves before we had to make our way back to Washington, DC, to pick up Gorbachev's ZiL limousines. Rather than sit by the pool or try out the rocky beach nearby, I determined this would be an excellent opportunity to test my rusty Spanish by venturing deep into the capital city.

I made my way to the hotel lobby and exchanged $20 for Cuban pesos. The government's official and completely arbitrary exchange rate was one peso for $1.33, making each of our pennies worth 3/4 of a centavo. During my escapades around town, I found I could get twenty pesos for a single dollar on the black market. What a difference! That made each penny of ours worth twenty centavos, almost twenty-seven times the official rate!

After exchanging the money, I ate breakfast in the hotel's restaurant and had a very polite conversation with my waiter, him speaking very broken English, and me trying out my re-energized Spanish on him.

As soon as he found out I was American, not Russian, he instantly became my friend. "*No nos gustan los Soviéticos,*" he told me.

"Why don't you like them?" I asked.

"*Son sucios con cabezas redondos, y no tienen dinero!*"

He was calling them dirty roundheads with no money. Did the visiting crews not pay their bills or something?

The hotel staff members all assumed I was a member of the Soviet aircrew, but when they found out I was an American, not only did they love me, but they wanted my all-powerful money — and they wanted to practice their English on me. This despite the constant barrage of propaganda on TV, radio, and billboards inculcating the evil of American capitalism.

Castro billboard Fight Against the Impossible

Radio Martí, with its mission to "provide a contrast to Cuban media and provide its listeners with an uncensored view of current events" had only been broadcasting for two years, but evidently, it had a positive effect.

To handle my breakfast bill, I tried to pay in pesos. "Ah, no!" said the waiter, waving the back of his hand outward in a display of disgust. "That's water! Need dollars!"

I felt disappointed that I had exchanged my money for nothing. But I said okay and offered him my government VISA credit card.

Again, I was rebuffed.

"How about a traveler's check?"

My attempt was rejected once more. "US not pay Cuba."

Finally, I got the message. Cuban money is so worthless and political strain so intense, that no money flows between our two countries.

I put up a good argument, in Spanish, with both the waiter and his supervisor. "This is ridiculous," I said. "I'm in Cuba, eating Cuban food at a Cuban hotel, and you won't accept Cuban pesos. That makes absolutely no sense! What if I don't have any dollars on me? Would you rather take my pesos or let me have the food for free?"

Of course, I was bluffing. They knew it, but I was miffed. I get like that sometimes. My daughters and wife always curl up in detached embarrassment when it happens in their presence, but they weren't here to witness this public display.

"I travel all over the world and exchange money into local denominations, and I come to this island and can't even pay for a meal with your own money."

They didn't relent. They weren't allowed to. Everyone knew pesos were worthless, and the only way the hotel could make ends meet was to demand foreign currency from foreigners. Or was it just Americanos? I didn't think to ask the Soviets how they paid. I just wanted to get on my way and enjoy a day among the locals. I finally paid for breakfast with the American cash I had on hand.

Sam felt as deep an interest as I did in exploring, but because there was no official American presence on the island, we first stopped by the Swiss Embassy to let them know what we were doing. The lady at the Embassy warned us against using the local bus system because it was so confusing. She didn't realize I had two years of experience bopping around big South American cities on public transportation. I could easily ask questions to figure out how to get where we wanted to go.

Ignoring her advice, we caught a random *guagua*, as they call their buses, to see where it would take us. At 6' 2" and with a lighter complexion than most Cubans, I immediately attracted attention. Students boldly came up and asked if I was American, mainly so they could practice their minimal English on me. It was fun. They were amazed to hear me speak their language, and soon I had quite a gaggle around me. I asked them simple questions:

"What do you think of Castro?"
"What do you know about America?"
"Do you get a good education here?"
"Do you have decent job opportunities?"
"Do your families eat well enough?"

The answers to those questions were as expected. Some loved Castro and others hated him. He helped the country overcome illiteracy but hurt the economy and job market tremendously. Because of that, poverty was rampant, and they knew life was better in the States.

The bus driver had the radio blaring with the usual propaganda, touting the greatness of Fidel and their Communist way of life for all riders to hear. News blurbs denigrated the United States, right in line with Castro's harsh anti-Americanism. Billboards sang out words like, "*Señores Imperialistas*, don't think we have any fear of you!" showing Uncle Sam growling at a calm Castro who was standing defiantly. It was quite humorous. I translated everything for Sam but didn't bother telling our admirers that my partner was an actual Uncle Sam!

As lunchtime approached, we jumped off the bus near a pizzeria. I found a place to get the full twenty pesos for a dollar, so I had plenty of dough on me. Now that we were far from the tourist traps, no one expected to be paid in dollars. The black-market rate made everything dirt cheap. As we sat down at the counter, I could sense people staring. One brave young man came up and sat beside me as he asked if I was *"Americano."*

"Sí, soy," I replied. With that, he blurted out his pent-up love of all things American in a machine gun flurry of questions. He fired his queries so fast that I couldn't answer before the next one came.

"What's it like in America?"

"How did you learn Spanish so well?"

"Do you like Cuba?"

"Is it easy to find a job in the US?"

"What's the best way to learn English?"

I answered the questions in similar short bursts, glorifying the United States and simultaneously telling them that their country was beautiful, without getting into a political discussion about the foibles of Communism. I loved that they seemed so enamored with the English language.

I paid what must have been about 20¢ US for two slices of vegetable pizza and a Fanta orange soda. Even with a sagging crust and cabbage overpowering all other ingredients, it tasted great. The conversation was good too. I walked away having learned that Cubans hate Russians, love Americans, and have no hope whatsoever of their own country ever coming out of economic ruin. They just happily live the only lives they know, raising their kids and looking for fun and fulfillment wherever they can find it.

Speaking of fun, I had one place I wanted to see. It was the only "famous" place I'd ever heard of in Havana: El Clúb Tropicana.[25] I asked a local which bus route would take us there.

Along our way to the Club, we tried to shop. I wanted to find souvenirs for my wife and kids and maybe the guys back at the office. But as we walked along a major street in what looked like the commercial district of town, Sam and I were shocked to see how few things were available for purchase.

Department store displays were extremely sparse. Instead of the fancy displays of clothing, jewelry and knick-knacks I was used to seeing all over the world, there was almost nothing. In one window that was several feet wide, I saw a roll of toilet paper, a single adjustable wrench, and a plunger to unclog a drain. Each small item was separated by a couple of empty feet. It must have been a hardware store, but there were no lights to detail even those minimal items on display. We didn't bother to go inside.

Instead, we looked for street vendors. There were very few. The T-shirts offered were flimsy and cheap. I couldn't find anything else, though, so I bought some in various sizes. I knew they'd shrink when washed, so I tried to guess which bigger size might end up being right for each of my girls. I was never much of a shopper, however, and I quickly realized that I was not going to improve that reputation among my household of women by bringing home cheap Cuban souvenirs. My shopping experience in Havana was pretty much over before it began.

---

25. I mistakenly thought the Tropicana was the place where Cuban-born Desi Arnaz, aka Ricky Ricardo, made his band famous. I didn't realize until later that the Tropicana Club in the *I Love Lucy* TV series was actually in the Bronx, New York. Oops! Goes to show you how TV can distort reality. Ricky Ricardo had nothing to do with this club in Havana.

We found some genuine Havana cigars, the kind I knew were very sought after by some of my compadres back at the office, so even though I don't smoke, I decided to buy a box and smuggle them back in my suitcase. I knew my boss would really like them!

By late afternoon, we found the Tropicana. It seemed barren and run-down, not the glitzy showplace I'd imagined. But there was a restaurant, and an early matinee, so we stayed to watch.

It wasn't impressive. The dancers' high kicks were about half as high as those performed by the Rockettes at Radio City Music Hall. The sparsity of the audience was also a surprise, and the show was interrupted twice by cloudbursts. Each time, the servers would come out, sop up the rain on our table, and the show would resume. It was a solid taste of culture, and we enjoyed our afternoon out.

With no one around to talk to, we returned to our dumpy hotel satisfied with our day's daring exploration. It had overall been a winner.

Chapter 9 - The Flag

Сделал дело—гуляй смело
"Did the job well – now go walk boldly"

12 December 1987, Saturday

The 3.7-hour return flight from Havana to Washington, DC, on Friday was uneventful, except for a couple of telling conversations with two different Soviet crew members.

First, the subject of theology came up with the navigator, Aleksei. I knew that religion did, in fact, exist in the Soviet Union, no matter how much the State tried to stifle it. One of the senior Shotgunners had Slavic roots and told me that his relatives still living there organized Russian Orthodox conferences. They smuggled their manuscripts to the United States to be printed, then smuggled them back as tracts for distribution.

But I was curious what Aleksei had to say. "*Yest' li religiya v vashey strane?*" Is there religion in your country?

"*Nyet, no ya pomnyu, kak moya babushka govorila o Boge.*" It barely exists now, he said. Everyone he knew was atheist, but he remembered his grandmother speaking of God.

"Do you believe there could be a God?" I continued.

"I've never thought much about it. We are taught from very young that there is no such thing."

"What did you think of your grandmother's beliefs?"

"I considered her to be old-fashioned, but I knew she sincerely believed. She was a wonderful woman, and I would never argue with her about it. We have plenty of Orthodox churches around, but mostly only elderly women attend. I did go with her once when I was very young. It's a good memory."

"I believe in God very strongly, like your grandmother. In the United States, most people do. In fact, religious freedom was one of the principles our country's government is based on. It's an extremely important concept to me and my family."

Suddenly Aleksei's demeanor changed. Instead of a hard-core refusal to consider the possibility of a God, he divulged knowledge of an organization within his country that aggressively promoted religion. "They wrote a book called *Christ in the Soviet Union*."

"They did? I'd sure love to read it." I never conceived that such an institution could exist within their godless system. "Can you tell me how to get a copy?"

Aleksei took my address and said he'd have one sent. Regrettably, I never received it.

He could never discuss such things with any of his peers because Soviets considered anyone who showed any inclination toward religion to have a psychological disorder.

Confirming we were on course, I made my way aft to the cargo area to mingle with the enlisted men, letting Sam handle the Shotgun seat in the upper cockpit. This whole trip, I'd been curious about the gun turret blatantly fashioned into the tail of the airplane. Though no gun barrels were protruding, it was obvious the entire section was meant to house rather large armaments. I later learned it was possible to install two twin-barrel 23 mm cannons in that area.

This aircraft handled materiel and troops, so why did it have a built-in space for a rear-facing crew member to handle rapid-fire weapons? I found the cargo master and tried to phrase my query:

"*Pochemu u vas zdes' oruzhiye?*"

He shrugged his shoulders uncomfortably. He knew he couldn't very well answer me straightforwardly, since I was an American and he was surrounded by his superiors. Instead, he came up with a pretty wild tale.

"The compartment is made for the navigator to check the flap position before landing." In a word, he lied. I was not inclined to push any further. He was just a pawn in a large and complicated bureaucratic chess game, and wasn't free to talk. He probably didn't even know any substantial details. Nor did he have any reason to reveal secrets to me, a complete stranger from his country's nemesis. Besides, the political officer was already eyeing me cautiously. I let it go, but it stayed on my mind.

Not until I did research for this book did I discover that the IL-76 wings could accommodate pylons for bomb deployment. A video released by the Russian Ministry of Defense showcases this warlike capability.[26]

Gun turret in tail. (No barrels protruded from any IL-76 I escorted, but the infrastructure was there.)

We remained overnight at Andrews AFB. The next morning, we loaded up the two ZiL limousines Gorbachev used during the just-completed summit. Slightly bent at the waist, my arms behind my back and hands clasped together, I gawked at one of them. These gorgeous Soviet-built automobiles strapped to the cargo bay reminded me of my dad's Lincoln Continentals. We had owned several. Each had a beautiful shimmering black-gray shine and all the luxury you'd expect from a limousine. The ZiLs sported plush leather seats, a handsome steering wheel, and a sleek instrument panel. This particular car was already two years old, but you wouldn't know it. The chrome sparkled, the wax finish was dazzling, and there wasn't a piece of chipped paint

---

26. youtu.be/kF0pqFJ2SuM

anywhere! It didn't have all the sweet curves of a modern Western luxury automobile, but it was certainly impressive in its masculine statement of bulky toughness and cool superiority.

The ZiL 41051[27] limo, an upgraded armored version of an earlier model, was only manufactured until 1985. They made only a few and used them exclusively during state parades and political summits like what the world had just witnessed. The limos were built under conditions of strict stealthiness and maintained in closed garages by a special division of the KGB. Anyone who had any involvement with them was sworn to secrecy.

Gorbachev's ZiL limousine

Each measured over 20.5 feet long and was fitted with bullet-proof windows and a powerful V-8 engine that gave them a top speed of 118 mph. A military plant in Kurgan, USSR, had built the limo's foundational armor, and the rest of the vehicle was constructed around that protective inner capsule. It sported dual ignition systems, one of which was for emergency use — much like the redundancy engineered into aircraft. All together, these limousines weighed a massive seven thousand pounds each, about

---

27. wikipedia.org/wiki/ZIL-4104

the same as an empty Learjet.

It's interesting to note that ZiL also built trucks, buses, armored personnel carriers, and even a racing car. They went bankrupt by 2013; perhaps that's why someone thought it an excellent investment to snatch up Gorby's & Yeltsin's 1989 inviolable limo, the ZiL 41052, for a cool $1.6 million in 2015.

One of the enjoyable sidelines of our escort duties was to swap whatnots with our counterparts. Before each trip, our supervisors encouraged us to purchase and bring along trinkets to trade with the Soviet crew members. They always showed interest in American gadgets, particularly military paraphernalia. In return, they'd generally offer us cheap pins or plastic wings; nothing valuable. From the Andrews AFB uniform store, we'd purchase a few sets of USAF pilot wings and a few other insignificant gizmos: a couple of sew-on patches, some stickers with unit emblems on them, and some inexpensive lapel pins. These items always came in handy, but I wasn't prepared for the most coveted barter I'd be asked to make.

Mr. Gorbachev's car had an attractive hammer and sickle banner hanging from the driver's side antenna. It was a miniature replica of the country's official flag and signaled undisputed ownership by the Premier. The subtle contrast of bright yellow emblems on a coquelicot red-orange background was a familiar symbol of the Soviet enterprise. They represented proletarian solidarity: the union of the peasantry (sickle) with the working class (hammer). The flag became a popular symbol of the Soviet Union at the end of the Russian Revolution (1917-1923). However, the use of those emblems as a calling card for workers to unite can be traced even further back to the previous century.[28]

---

28. i.e. the Chilean peso of 1895

The copilot, Anatoliy, took a break from his cockpit seat and came down to stretch his legs while I was still admiring the limousine.

"Glenn," he said, "I want you to have a wonderful souvenir from the historic meeting of our two heads of state."

"That's very kind of you, Anatoliy," I replied. "What do you have in mind?"

He took three steps toward the left side of the ZiL, then gingerly slipped the Soviet flag off the antenna. "Here," he said, holding out the silky cloth atop both of his outstretched palms. "You take this home."

Shocked, I exclaimed, "Oh, no! I can't take the flag off of Secretary Gorbachev's limousine. That would get us both in trouble!"

The small 7 X 14 Soviet flag

I glanced around for Graysuit. Surely he wouldn't approve of this. It wasn't Anatoliy's to give, and I didn't want to be accused of stealing.

Yet Anatoliy continued to push. "No, my friend. You have provided us a great service. My boss would be happy for you to have it."

What a quandary! It was my very first Shotgun mission, and even though I had been briefed about the customary trinket-swapping, I was not prepared for them to present such a meaningful piece of US/Soviet history. I was unsure of what to do. However, he continued to assure me this was a perfectly typical offering.

"I have nothing of such great value to offer you in exchange," I finally muttered, as I subtly tried to slide the flag back onto the antenna.

He stopped me. "You must take it. I insist. You can give me your flight cap if it would make you feel better." He pointed to the hat hanging halfway out of my flight suit's right pant leg pocket. So that's what motivated his kindness!

An Air Force officer's hat, known as a garrison cap, has a couple of unique characteristics. First, its silver braid edging distinguishes an officer from an enlisted person. Second, a badge pinned to its forward front left side clearly specifies the rank of the wearer. I was a Captain, so the emblem, made of silver metal, resembled a train track with two spars holding the rails together at each end.

 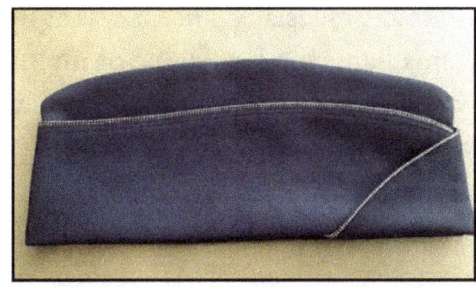

Pilots regularly slid them into a leg pocket of their green flight suit. I owned several of these caps because I regularly misplaced them and it never hurt to have a spare handy. Walking outside in uniform without head gear was a *faux pas* and required one to "escape and evade" the condescending judgment of other military members. In this scenario, however, giving up my hat was no big deal; I'd be traveling home from Gander in civilian clothing anyway and wouldn't need it. We didn't wear them while working in and around airport ramps due to the danger of FOD. Still, I felt like I would commit an unforgivable act of treachery by taking the flag. I wondered if it was a test of my integrity or part of the *glasnost* openness of the new Soviet regime.

"What will your Secretary think when he sees this missing?" I asked.

"It will not be missed at all. They will quickly replace it with an identical one."

With calculated zeal, he pressed the prized flag against my rib cage. Despite my resistance, it was obvious I could not get out of the deal. Seeing no one around to object, and rationalizing that it was indeed a fair trade, I finally relented, stuffing the unexpected bonus into my zippered chest pocket.

Then I reached down, pulled my flight cap out of my leg pocket, and handed it to Anatoliy. His face lit up, making plain his utter delight in winning this coveted reward. He had made a very good trade, especially since it was at no expense of his own!

That small antenna flag is one of my most prized possessions from my military career. I proudly display it in my office in a large frame along with all of my unit patches. Thankfully, I never got implicated in a crime for swiping it.

Eight months after our return from this, my very first Shotgun trip, all fifteen USAF escorts received the Air Force Achievement Medal for our roles in successfully handling these high-level diplomatic flights. The citation that accompanied the award certainly contained a measure of hyperbole in referring to our "outstanding professional skill, judgment, and diplomacy" — our place in history was extremely minimal — but being formally recognized helped me understand that my efforts to become part of the Shotgun program had been very worthwhile. Further, it shaped my confidence that I certainly "did the job well" and could now "go walk boldly" in my future performance as a Shotgun pilot.

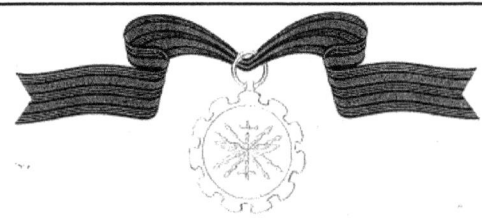

DEPARTMENT OF THE AIR FORCE

THIS IS TO CERTIFY THAT

THE AIR FORCE ACHIEVEMENT MEDAL

HAS BEEN AWARDED TO

CAPTAIN ▓▓▓▓▓▓▓▓

FOR

OUTSTANDING ACHIEVEMENT
15 NOVEMBER 1987 TO 11 DECEMBER 1987

ACCOMPLISHMENTS

Captain ▓▓▓▓▓▓▓▓ distinguished himself as Safety Escort Officer in support of the United States and Union of Soviet Socialist Republic Intermediate Nuclear Forces Treaty summit talks. His outstanding professional skill, judgment and diplomacy aided immeasurably in the successful completion of these high visibility missions. Despite marginal weather, Soviet inexperience with United States Air Traffic procedures, and constantly changing schedules, he insured that all the Soviet support flights were completed smoothly and safely, with no operational or diplomatic incidents.

GIVEN UNDER MY HAND THIS   14TH   DAY OF   JULY   1988

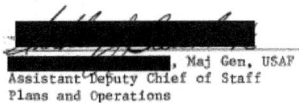

▓▓▓▓▓▓▓▓, Maj Gen, USAF
Assistant Deputy Chief of Staff
Plans and Operations

Chapter 10 - The General

Поживём – увидим
"We will live – we will see"

7 July 1990, Wednesday[29]

"Man, it's colder than Siberia down here," I said in my best elementary Russian as I introduced myself to the Soviet two-star General early in our flight. Since I had no cockpit duties for another hour, I'd gone to look around down below. I didn't think to record the name of this distinguished-looking gentleman, nor could I discern a good reason for his presence on this trip. Suffice it to say he was a bigwig in the USSR military hierarchy. Enlisted folks and lower-ranked officers make up the bulk of any military force, so having a general officer on board was significant.

"Да," he agreed.

Our lumbering cargo plane was support to the two modern supersonic MiG-29 jet fighters flying alongside us to star in US air shows. The famed Cold War was waning and air show organizers around the country begged for the alluring sight of Soviet flying machinery in action. An up-close and personal look at a MiG-29 Fulcrum fighter was virtually unknown up to now, although aviation writers had touted the reputation of the highly praised aircraft for years. To watch these famous enemy aircraft slip the surly bonds and put on dazzling shows of maneuverability, speed, and prowess would be a real treat for

---

29. Somehow, I have misconstrued the actual dates of this episode, but the experience portrayed is accurate.

thousands.

With four days of demonstrations at Kalamazoo, Michigan, behind them, the fighter jets now headed for Minot AFB, North Dakota, for refueling.

A mere Captain, I was five full ranks below this Russian counterpart who sat downstairs amid pallets of spare aircraft parts. The cargo didn't mind temperatures in the low sixties, but the cargo compartment was way too frigid and uncomfortable for any of the passengers, or pax, aboard, let alone someone of such high rank. I thought I knew just what the General was thinking as he sat sideways, shivering uncomfortably on troop seats made of 2-inch-wide belt-like nylon straps rather than in a nice, cushioned, forward-facing airline seat. *I put up with a lot of crap to see America. Maybe this wasn't such a great idea!*

Military service often calls for personal sacrifice, and this flight included some of that, even for such a VIP. I wondered what roles the General played as he climbed the organizational ladder of the Soviet Military Air Forces (VVS[30]). Had he, in his earlier years, sat alert with nuclear bombs strapped to the wings of his fighter, poised to respond at a moment's notice to do serious harm to my country? Did he suspect that I, a U-2 pilot, had flown my plane close enough to his borders to collect strategic imagery and communications for my national leaders?

The general propelled the conversation further. "*Ya kak raz sobiralsya podoyti i poprosit' vas, rebyata, razogret!* (I was just about to come up to ask you guys to turn up the heat!) Even these thick Russian furs aren't keeping me warm!"

Nodding in agreement, I returned to the cockpit. Though he was "the enemy," I felt for the guy. Most of the pax on this flight worked only while we were on the ground; they had no function

---

30. Voenno-Vozdushnye Sily

while airborne, and there was no room for them in the cramped, but warm, upper level of the two-tiered aircraft. The cockpit was reserved for trained airmen who performed vital in-flight functions. Indeed, we lower-ranking crew members were all cozy in our padded chairs with the windows draped around us refracting the sunlight and warming the cockpit of the IL-76.

I absently closed the bulkhead door behind me, climbed a short set of stairs, and relayed his not-so-subtle message to the aircrew.

"Hey, turn up the heat in the back. Your General is freezing!" The flight engineer seemed busy, unresponsive.

"Comrades! *Rebyata, razogret'!* " I repeated, though I'm sure it didn't come out right. This time, I got the standard brush-off normally reserved for a petulant child.

My level of experience with the horrendously difficult Russian language boiled down to a single conversational area that I facetiously called "aviationese." I couldn't strike up a dialog with the general or the crew about their golf game or ask more than basic details about their wives or children. Now, despite my best efforts in their language, I finally had to resort to brazen English slang. "Your general down in the cargo seats is freezing his gonads off. Can you zap some more heat his way?"

I heard the flight engineer mumble something in Russian that I couldn't quite understand, then saw him quickly and absentmindedly, as if bothered, reach up to his massive control panel and turn a small dial up a notch. I assumed he finally followed through with my request by mixing a little more bleed air from the hot engines into the cavernous cargo bay.

Satisfied, I donned my David Clark headset to monitor our progress and ensure we were on the approved track while strictly adhering to Air Traffic Control (ATC) guidance and all FAA rules.

The crew and I easily forgot our status as military opponents. We all had a passion for aviation, and we each had families at home to love and provide for. At our level in society, we could easily discount the inter-governmental misunderstandings that had created the uneasy political situation feeding the Cold War for the last forty years.

Or could we? Was there an unseen goal for this trip? Why was there a General Officer on board who had no apparent purpose? My background and training sent such thoughts bouncing around my brain.

"What does KRSPY mean?" Sergei asked, jerking my thoughts back to reality. Fascinated by our National Airspace System (NAS), he had the most recent Enroute High navigation chart spread before him, folded to show our current flight path. As he pointed to one of the hundreds of intersections-in-the-sky identified on the map, it once again occurred to me that whoever developed these charts must amuse themselves by making up unique monikers.

"It's trying to spell 'Krispy' with just five letters," I answered. Although there are often good reasons for the shortened names of such junctions, sometimes they're completely made up by fun-loving cartographers.

I pointed to another intersection called "MILTO" in Wisconsin. "This point is named for a nearby town named Millston. Computerized navigation systems require all airway intersections to contain exactly five letters. Here, they took letters from the town below to identify a spot directly overhead."

"We're going too FAR," I added, pausing slightly to see if Sergei caught my very poor joke. Humor is hard to translate between languages — especially my corny puns in aviationese!

He just looked at me quizzically.

I repeated, "We're going to F A R," this time pointing to an airport along our route of flight: Fargo, North Dakota. Since airports have three-letter identifiers to distinguish them from intersections, Fargo's Hector International was annotated as "FAR" on the map.

I showed him another one of my favorites, hundreds of miles to the west.

"Look at this," I said, tapping the map. "CZI is a navigational aid (NAVAID) in Wyoming. It's named for a creek near its position called 'Crazy Woman.'" W e both laughed. We were fast becoming more comfortable with each other, building on commonalities rather than focusing on lingering strains between our two cultures.

The Radio Operator (RO) sat with his back to us across the narrow aisle. As the fifth and lowest paid member of the flight crew, his job as liaison between the pilots and ATC was especially important. Most ROs spoke English quite well. I noticed that this particular radioman had considerable trouble understanding controllers who often transmitted instructions in

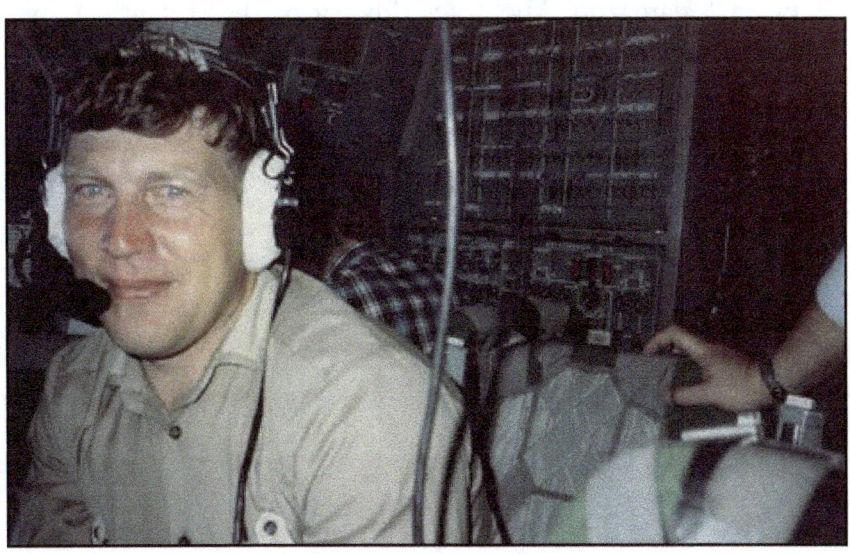

Soviet IL-76 Radio Operator

a fast, turbulent clip. He occasionally turned and tapped me on the arm with his shoulders raised and hands upturned in a questioning gesture, indicating he didn't understand what the controller had just said. Sometimes he entirely missed a call intended for us. My long experience as an instructor pilot made me very attuned to student pilots missing calls like that, so I was ready to intervene quickly when necessary.

Since everyone in the cockpit wore the old-style bulky Mickey Mouse ear headsets and heard all the calls, I could easily clarify things for him. I'd been flying these same airways for years, and radio communications were second nature to me. I would often just make the needed reply for him in order to speed up the back-and-forth dialog with ATC. There's no time to dilly-dally when dealing with the rapid-fire comms from a controller managing a dozen or more aircraft at once.

"Rawjer," I butted in now. "Aeroflot 223 going over to Minneapolis Center on 134.25."

Just a routine frequency change.

From Kalamazoo, Michigan, this leg of the trip was a 763-mile jaunt to the northwest. I started to review the upcoming approach procedure to Minot AFB, but hardly got started before I was suddenly interrupted. We were about to get intimately familiar with an unplanned airport.

Chapter 11 - Stone Cold

Друг познаётся в беде́
"A friend in need is a friend indeed"

7 July 1990, Wednesday (continued)

Even if you've never served in the military, it won't shock you to learn that Generals are used to getting what they want, when they want it.

It was no surprise, then, that none of those passengers huddled in the frigid cargo hold gave it a second thought when the General, dressed in full Soviet uniform regalia, casually stood from his incommodious cold perch to stroll toward the bulkhead door that separated the cargo bay from the cockpit. Chilled and bored stiff, he wanted to mingle with the aircrew and maybe get a better perspective of this new and mysterious country he was overflying for the first time. The few small porthole windows in the aft section allowed precious little view of the ground below.

He certainly had every right to visit us up top, and his presence would have been a welcome break from the monotony of a long two-and-a-half-hour cruise. At an altitude of 28,000' MSL,[31] the in-flight task load was much lighter than during the hectic takeoff-and-climb phase or the always-busy descent and approach, which was followed by the toughest part of any flight — the hoped-for squeaky smooth landing. Now was the best possible time for a visitor.

Behind that closed bulkhead door rose a simple, unadorned metal stairway that protruded into the beehive of the second-

---

31. Above Mean Sea Level

level cockpit. As the General nonchalantly reached for the door handle to make his grand entrance, he was oblivious — as was the crew — to the fact that a slight pressure differential had insidiously built up over the last hour or more of flight, ever since I had shut the bulkhead door.

Perhaps this particular flight engineer wasn't accustomed to having passengers on a traditionally cargo-only aircraft. Or maybe he didn't realize that the door dividing the two main areas of the aircraft had been closed and latched. Whatever the reason, he failed to keep the pressurization equal between both compartments.

That slight disparity set us all up for a big surprise. The pressure difference wasn't huge — the system wouldn't allow for too great a divergence, so it was likely as little as two pounds per square inch — but it was enough.

B-O-O-M! A thunderous blast reverberated through the entire aircraft.

My body jerked, my heart skipped a beat, and my ears popped as the air pressure equalized between the compartments. Everyone upstairs immediately looked at each other with raised eyebrows in a non-verbal, "*What was THAT???!!!*"

As the one sitting closest to the stairs that led to the lower level, I yelled over the ringing in my ears, "I'll go see what's up!"

I ripped off my headset and took two quick leaps to the stairwell. Looking down, I saw our VIP general sprawled out limply at the base of the spiral staircase, his cap toppled onto the floor, his body slumped in a tussled heap of toneless muscle.

Ever so gingerly, moving so as not to plop on top of him, I lowered myself and found him completely unconscious, a pool of bright red blood oozing from his forehead. *What in the world!!*

I sprung back up the ladder and, as calmly as my adrenaline allowed, explained to the Soviet aircraft commander that his

General was lying comatose at the bottom of the stairs and desperately needed medical attention.

I didn't attempt first-aid for fear I'd further complicate the scene. I wanted to be certain that no one could surmise that I, an American, had anything to do with the injury or death of a Soviet superior officer. That might create an international incident!

While one of the crew took it upon himself to render care for his high-ranking comrade, I flew into action, put on my headset and mashed the radio transmit button.

"Mayday, Mayday, Mayday," I barked into the microphone. "Minneapolis Center, this is Aeroflot 223. We've got a medical emergency on board and require immediate sequencing to Fargo International Airport."

"Rawjer, Aeroflot 223, understand you are declaring an emergency; turn left heading three-zero-zero degrees, descend at pilot's discretion to Flight Level (FL) 250."

"Three-zero-zero degrees and leaving FL 280 for FL 250, Aeroflot 223. Request you have an ambulance meet us at the airplane upon arrival. We have a foreign national VIP on board who is unconscious with a bleeding head wound."

"Copy that, Aeroflot 223. We have cleared all traffic ahead; you have priority into Fargo International. Can we be of any further assistance?"

"Rawjer, Minneapolis. Request you notify FAA International of our emergency. This is a Constant Shotgun special diplomatic flight and they need to be made aware of the situation. Thanks."

That was all I could do for now. Everyone was in high gear, knowing it was vital that we get down fast.

I was no longer near the accident scene, and I remained unaware of the General's current condition. *Was he getting worse? Were they able to stop the bleeding? He's not DEAD, is he, for heaven's sake?* All I could think of was the need to get him to the hospital.

Once I'd told the crew they had a man down, they seemed to immediately understand the cause of the accident. It almost seemed they'd experienced a mismatched pressure situation before.

The BOOM we'd all felt rumble through our bodies had been a mix of horrific sounds all muddled into one. A natural thunderclap developed when the two separate systems of air energetically came together as the cockpit entryway handle unlatched. Internal pressures instantly equalized, and all our ears underwent an involuntary valsalva action. The sound of the door's edge smacking the VIP squarely across the forehead added to the tumult. I'm certain the raucous yelp we heard during the commotion related to the surprise and pain of it all.

I couldn't understand the barrage of Russian dialog being rapidly flung about, but I got the distinct impression that the flight engineer was being rather fiercely reprimanded right on the spot for allowing the pressure differential to develop. Causing injury to a General Officer was certain to create further repercussions for that unfortunate crew member, though I was never privy to any specific measures taken.

I learned the IL-76 Candid could accommodate parachute troops, so a closed bulkhead door allowed the cockpit to stay pressurized while the parachutists exited at the rear of the fuselage. The design was useful for those types of operations, but such a capability was completely superfluous on most flights.

As a team, we got the airplane on the ground safely and expeditiously. The promised ambulance was right there waiting, lights flashing, sirens blaring. They made haste to get our venerable General to the local hospital.

Fargo was a joint-use airfield, used by both civilians and military, so the rest of us filed into the Air National Guard base operations lounge to await word of his prognosis. We didn't know what to say to each other because everyone was so concerned. It was almost like accidentally hitting your mother in the head while swinging a practice bat — what can you say? "Sorry" doesn't cut it, and nothing deeper or more meaningful came to anyone's mind. It seemed as if everyone felt it was their fault: one passenger felt he shouldn't have let the General leave his seat; a crew member worried that he'd not secured the bulkhead door open so that it couldn't close; the flight engineer stewed because he hadn't noticed the pressure differential building. It was all gloom and doom during that wait. I myself fretted that, as the safety escort, I'd allowed such an influential guest to get hurt on his maiden voyage to our country! After all, that was one of my primary duties — to ensure the well-being of these honored patrons.

I made a couple of quick calls to my boss and FAA International, the office that oversaw Shotgun flights. After explaining the situation, I asked them to notify Aeroflot officials and the Soviet military hierarchy. I promised to update them as soon as we got any word.

Almost three hours passed. We cleaned out the vending machines in the lounge area, snacking to pass the time. Many of us began nodding off in our uncomfortable parlor chairs, still unsure of the outcome.

Finally, we saw a hospital van approaching. In a wave of relief, we watched as the wounded superior officer stepped down onto the sidewalk, once again under his own power. A broad, thick, white bandage adorned his forehead, carefully wrapped.

And what was this? He was all smiles! As he walked into the ops lounge to greet us, to the total surprise of everyone, he passed right by the aircraft commander and other crewmen and headed straight to me! The broad grin on his face was difficult to comprehend under the circumstances until he grabbed me in a big Soviet bear hug and exclaimed,

"*Спасибо, Спасибо, Спасибо! Вы спасли мою жизнь!*" (*Thank you, thank you, thank you! You saved my life!*)

I was perplexed. I hadn't saved his life at all! My only role in the whole affair was to take over the radios, declare an emergency, and get us priority routing and an immediate descent while calling for an ambulance to meet us. How did he even know of my involvement? He had been knocked out!

Together, the bandaged General, the Russian flight crew, and my Shotgun partner and I continued with the rest of our three-day trip while the General continually praised me at every turn and now considered me his best friend.

For years, I have contemplated why he felt, and expressed, such profound gratitude. Of course, I never saw an official medical report. Could it be he was told by a doctor that a longer delay might have produced a far worse result? I highly doubt that — his recovery was so quick and complete that I can only imagine that his flesh wound was superficial and any concussion minor. After all, he was not even kept overnight for observation.

No, I have since concluded that his heart was so full, not because of a life saved, but because of the earlier human interaction of one man to another as I tried to get him warmed up. It unexpectedly transformed me from adversary to friend.

My spirit, too, was relieved that instead of becoming an international brouhaha, this airborne mishap proved to strengthen and solidify the developing brotherhood of two nations who had long been staunch rivals.

As we went our separate ways at the end of the road later that week, I distinctly remember catching the eye of the suspicious, quiet man in the Armani suit — the KGB "Graysuit." In those eyes, I thought I saw a softening as well. Was it toward me? Or hopefully, toward the entire American system? Maybe he now viewed this strangely different society as something more

Tech Tab #2: Pressurization

The flight engineer of a 20th-century cargo aircraft has one unique function that is fully automated in today's passenger airlines. The skin of an aircraft acts very much like a tin can, creating a protective cocoon for fragile human bodies being hurled through space. The untenable environment surrounding the plane at 35,000' above mean sea level (MSL) lacks essential life-preserving factors such as adequate oxygen, pressurization, and heat. Within the troposphere, the atmospheric layer we fly in, temperatures can dip to as low as -59°C! But even more fatal to our flimsy mortal frames is the lack of atmospheric pressure at those altitudes. The atmosphere can be thought of as layers of blankets on your bed. The higher you go, the fewer blankets there are on top of you. Thus, the force that "pushes" vital oxygen into every single living cell diminishes substantially as you climb. At sea level, 14.7 pounds of pressure per square inch (psi) forces oxygen into your entire system. At a typical cruise altitude of 35,000', that pressure is reduced to less than 4 psi — not enough to oxygenate your life-

capable, more sensitive than he'd allowed himself to believe.

And you know what? I finally saw in him a father, husband, and son who loved as I loved.

---

sustaining organs.

Airplanes that carry passengers are required by regulation to maintain a cabin altitude of no greater than 8,000' MSL by pressurizing the interior. This provides approximately 11 psi of pressure. Included with the outside air that continually refreshes cabin air, the system also uses engine bleed air to not only pressurize the compartment, but to add heat to counter the unbearable outside temperature. Today's Western-built aircraft don't include manual crew controls that would even allow a pressurization differential to build between compartments. Safety measures include blow-out panels in the bulkhead to prevent just such an occurrence. In 1971, when the IL-76 first flew, the Soviets saw no reason to condition the air in the cargo compartment with that much heat and pressure when there was no living entity in the back. In these aircraft, the bulkhead that divides the cockpit from the cargo area allows differing pressures to be maintained in flight if needed for parachute drops, for instance.

Chapter 12 - World's Largest Aircraft

Глаза разбегаютсяе
"Eyes wide open"

Antonov 225 - World's Largest Airplane

16 December 1990, Sunday

During the build-up to Desert Storm, I covered a two-month assignment monitoring Saddam Hussein's every move from the cockpit of the high-flying U-2.[32] It had been a stressful few months based in Saudi Arabia, and I was glad to be going home to RAF Alconbury in England.

As I climbed down the ladder from the Dragon Lady's cockpit after landing, I was met by my ecstatic family of girls. These five precious souls meant the world to me, and I'd missed them as I fought for freedom in a far away and insecure country.

We loved the years spent in England and traveled extensively in our big American Chevrolet Astro van. From Peterborough,

---

32. Called the TR-1 while based in Britain, the name change was to conceal the fact that the infamous U-2 spy plane operated from their bases. "TR" stood for "Tactical Reconnaissance."

we visited Wales, Scotland, France, Germany, Italy, Switzerland, and Austria. We put our girls in English primary schools, where they quickly absorbed the Brits' delightful accent. Even the church we attended was all-British, and we made many wonderful and lifetime friends.

My family greeted me as I returned from Saudi Arabia

Within a month of my return, we received orders to report to our new duty station in Virginia by the end of January 1991. With a few Shotgun trips already under my belt as "guest help," I was now being assigned to the project full time as the program's operations officer, responsible for scheduling and coordinating escorts for every flight.

I'll always be grateful to Colonel Al Westrom, the man who hired me for the job. He and his gracious wife, Judy, welcomed my family by inviting us into their home soon after our arrival. I was impressed with their warmth, Al's deep, commanding voice, and his extensive collection of model airplanes standing in a tall glass case in his family room. Though I was a mere Captain, he minimized our difference in rank by setting me at ease with his comfortable leadership style. He was always full of encouragement.

My predecessor, Major Pete Shockey, was moving on to his next flying assignment in the KC-10 Extender. I'd grilled Pete months earlier on the details of the job before agreeing to attempt it.

"What's the availability of base housing?"

"It should be easy to get because the engineering school on Ft. Belvoir is closing."

The military housing allowance (BAQ) for those who lived off base was $900 per month. I analyzed the situation and found we could afford a mortgage at that rate and get a house more suitable for my large family. We'd break even on our budget, build equity, and avoid forfeiting the BAQ money.

"Is there language training available?"

"Yes. A Russian tutor comes to the unit once or twice a week to work with us."

While this may have been helpful during Pete's tenure, it didn't benefit me much. The frequency of escort trips increased in the following years as the Soviet Union began to disintegrate, and I wasn't home often enough to take advantage.

5 March 1991, Tuesday

Life became a whirlwind. We spent nearly a month in a cramped TLF (Temporary Lodging Facility) on Ft. Belvoir, then moved into our new house in Dale City, Virginia. The van we borrowed from a friend while awaiting the arrival of ours from England broke down on us at least twice. Pam was eight months pregnant, and our four daughters began attending an unfamiliar elementary school, attempting to make new friends mid-year.

As for me, I had no choice but to hit my crushing new full-time job running, suddenly managing the nuts and bolts of the complicated Shotgun program. There were only two of us full-timers who wore pilot wings, but we had access to about thirty part-time pilots or navigators we could call upon as needed to support the missions, pulling them from other active duty or reserve flying units.

Two huge benefits came with the transition to full-time. First, I was given diplomatic, or "Dip" status, a big step up from both my traditional tourist and my official passports. This new passport would make entries to and departures from Moscow and other exotic places much easier, giving me quick access to necessary visas and extending valuable exemptions from customs red tape.

Professionally, it was a great honor. "Blanket" orders were another bennie. They should have been called "blank" orders because they were so wide open — I could effectively write my own. Military orders generally direct the member to a specific place at a precise time by means of a designated mode of transportation. Fund cites limit expenditures on lodging, transportation, and *per diem*.[33] Airmen often use printed orders to obtain military rates at hotels and airlines and to receive needed legal protection or professional attention in a foreign country.

High-tension priorities in this chaotic new job were staggering, and deftly juggling work, family, home, and church responsibilities at home, family and church made life's balancing act nearly impossible. I felt extreme stress on all sides.

The world, too, was in commotion. The ground war in Iraq began and ended the week before I jumped into the job full blast. Intense negotiations were underway between Soviet and US nuclear arms teams. President George H. W. Bush wanted even

---

33. The daily amount allowed for meals and incidentals for the locale where the job is to be performed.

more sweeping arms reductions than the historic Reagan/Gorbachev Intermediate-Range Nuclear Forces (INF) Treaty of late 1987. Whereas Reagan had effectively eliminated intermediate- and short-range ballistic missiles, Mr. Bush wanted to dramatically reduce ICBMs (Intercontinental Ballistic Missiles) with the new START[34] Treaty.

Amid all this turmoil, I had to pack to leave my expectant wife and jump on a Pan Am passenger jet for my first look at the Capital of the Union of Soviet Socialist Republics.

6 March 1991, Wednesday

Most of my Shotgun flights had started either from Gander or Anchorage, but not this trip. This trip began in Moscow. I'd long dreamt of the day I'd get to see the Soviet Union. I practically shivered in anticipation to get my first look at the most mysterious of all world capitals. As a bonus, I was going to fly as an extra crew member aboard the world's largest airplane, the Antonov 225 *Mriya*, a pilot's dream!

After four years of escorting Russian aircraft, I finally had the chance to travel to the alien land of our Cold War enemy and experience this phenom of a flying machine. It was as if I had won the grand prize.

My partner for this trip was Major Frank Peluso, an old hand at this business. A few years ago, he'd held the ops officer job I was just now stepping into. A fluent Russian speaker, he'd since served as the Assistant Air Attaché in Moscow, the very job I was aiming for. He was the perfect guy to give me the 'gouge' I needed to find my way into that position.

After a long delay retrieving our visas from the Soviet

---

34. https://tinyurl.com/STARTreduce

Consulate, Frank and I rushed over to Washington, DC's, Reagan National Airport for a quick hop to JFK in New York, only to wait four hours for our connecting flight outbound.

As Pan Am flight #30[35] descended into Moscow, butterflies seized my stomach. While passing through sparse, scattered clouds, it hit me that I was about to land in territory I'd trained to fight. The lights below us could have belonged to any big city, but I knew better. This was the heart of the Big, Bad, Soviet Bear.

I wondered how I should handle my first face-to-face encounter with the country, the culture, and most importantly, its common people, some of whom I would soon be greeting. My studies while based in England had earned me a master's degree in international relations with an emphasis in Soviet history. I'd read of the brash brutality of the Gulag prisons, the ruthless reigns of the czars, and the horrible displacements and worse suffered by Soviet Jews. I knew something of the country's bitter, harsh winters, the frequent and famines endured by their people over the centuries, and the godlessness of their current form of government.

Antonov Design Bureau advertising banner

With my limited knowledge of this enemy's history, language, and lifestyle, would I be able to communicate with or relate to them in any way? Why had we become enemies in the first place, after having joined forces in World War II just four

---

35. https://youtu.be/KkTTgaTKm5Q

decades before?

Should I hate them?

Seventeen years earlier, I had landed in Buenos Aires, Argentina, as a young missionary for the Church of Jesus Christ of Latter-day Saints. I had been eager to embark upon a two-year adventure in a new land, but apprehensive about confronting the unknown world of Argentina.

Sure enough, as soon as I stepped out onto the dirt streets near my first apartment in a suburb of Buenos Aires, the reality of a foreign and unfamiliar land slammed my psyche.

I had studied Spanish for five years before arriving in Argentina, yet the porteños I met might just as well have been speaking Chinese. Little children laughed at my accent as I tried to speak their native tongue, and I understood nothing they said in their fast-paced dialect. Compounding the rift between us, I quickly and critically noticed the odd Argentine ways of doing things — nothing was warm, natural, or comfortable. Most people didn't have cars, they ate strange foods that my stomach rejected, and there were no dishwashers or swimming pools.

I felt so out of place those first three months. In my culture-shocked and somewhat prideful soul, I asked myself, "*Why is this country so strange? Why do they do everything so differently? Can't they see we have the better way? What is wrong with these people?*"

Then I had an experience that changed my view of foreigners forever.

La Pampa, the Argentine Wild West, was famous for its South American cowboys, the *gauchos*. While traveling to the capital, the long-distance bus my mission companion and I were on stopped somewhere to pick up more passengers. I had chosen a seat near the back by a window and opened it to move some air around the stuffy cabin.

Straight away, I became aware of a little girl reaching up to my window from outside the bus with her hand outstretched, asking for a *moneda* (coin). I must have been having a bad day because at first, the hardness of my heart surfaced. I thought, *"Why should I, a missionary who has no means of income, give you a coin? Your parents should be supporting you!"*

Please don't hate me for that selfish thought; I'm embarrassed it ever entered my mind. But then I looked into her eyes. They were big, soft, and brown, just like my nine-year-old sister Rachael's. This young girl was even her same age and size. Suddenly, the Argentine girl transformed into my little sister!

By that time, I hadn't seen my cherished little sibling for a full year. I burst into tears and reached into my pocket to find a little money to give this needy girl ... and the bus pulled away. The image of the tiny girl standing there, hand extended, with expectant, needy, big, brown eyes, still lingers and saddens me greatly because that opened hand was still empty! I hadn't had time to give her anything before the bus lurched forward.

The only difference between this Argentine girl and my sister was their circumstances of birth: poverty versus privilege. She was born speaking Spanish, while our native tongue was the more universal English. She was likely born in a shanty on a muddy, bumpy road, while Rache was born in a sterile, air-conditioned hospital attended by the best medical care the world offered.

From that moment on, I saw every person I contacted in a different light. In some, I'd see my blood brothers; in others, I could pick out features of my parents or grandparents or any of the friends I'd ever loved. Despite our differences, all people of all nations morphed into my bona fide brothers and sisters — family. I didn't have to take the time to get to know them individually before I loved them, because I instantly saw they were God's children, just like me.

The flashback faded. Back in the "now" of 1991, I held to that memory as we touched down in that other world of the Cold War Soviet Union. I had a sneaky hunch that I might find Russians, Ukrainians, Uzbeks, and Turkmenistanis warmer and more personal than I had previously considered. Perhaps my tough and unyielding soul could finally grasp the most important lesson that the Supreme Power had been trying to instill in me throughout my entire existence—that God is the Father of all; that we are all literally brothers and sisters on the same journey.

Destruction of the AN-225

Tech Tab #3

Thursday, 24 February 2022

Dubbed "*Mriya*" ("Dream" in Ukrainian), the AN-225 was an aeronautical marvel engineered in the 1980s by the Antonov Design Bureau in Ukraine to transport the Soviet space shuttle *Buran*. When their space plane mission was scrubbed, the colossal airship ultimately became the world's premier vehicle for handling outsized freight. With six massive turbofan engines, the Mriya could carry half a million pounds of cargo, almost twice as much as a Boeing 747. Thirty-two wheels were needed to handle that kind of weight upon landing. From nose to tail and wingtip to wingtip, this monstrosity of a machine was as long and as wide as a football field. Only one was ever one created.

The Mriya's maiden voyage was on December 21, 1988, only two years before I had the great privilege of flying it. I flew it again later that same year, in November 1991.

Those flights were highlights of my aviation career, and when the news first broke of the AN-225's destruction by Russian forces invading Ukraine in 2022, my heart sank. That single plane was the one-and-only copy of the world's largest aircraft ever. It had been undergoing maintenance in a hangar at Hostomel Airfield near Kyiv when the Russians attacked the airfield.

AN-225 bombed by Russia, February 2022

Chapter 13 - Children of Chernobyl

Хорошие вещи приходят в больших упаковках
"Good things come in large packages"

6 March 1991, Wednesday (continued)

The Boeing 747 touched down, and the reality of Moscow unfolded. People who looked like me bustled around the airport. En route to the hotel, I saw women buying groceries, men heading out after a day of work or school, others playing with their children. Though their dress and surroundings were somewhat different, the similarities between us absorbed my attention.

We arrived in Moscow at 1025L and stayed with the Puseys, Frank's friends from his attaché assignment. Mr. Pusey was away on business, but his gracious wife and two children took good care of us, giving us a delicious meal and comfortable beds. Their home on the US Embassy grounds was modern, with many of the conveniences of American upper-class living. They received non-perishable groceries from American military commissaries via a regular provisioning flight from Germany.

We went shopping at the Ukrainian Hotel, which, at 676 feet, was the tallest hotel, not only in Russia, but in all of Europe. At its grand opening in 1957, it had been the tallest in the entire world, holding that distinction until 1976. One of Moscow's famed "Seven Sisters" skyscrapers, it had been commissioned by Joseph Stalin.

Frank kept calling the Soviet Air Ministry to get the required rendezvous information for our return trip. After several attempts, he finally got the straight scoop, because they didn't have a solid plan. He was used to having to push hard to extract details in this culture. In the end, they asked us to meet at 0500L the next morning in front of the Embassy.

The Soviet way of life intrigued me, but as much as I'd studied Moscow and imagined it, I wasn't prepared for the bleakness of experiencing it in person. The lack of basic freedoms and goods that I took so much for granted was obvious, and it hurt. It seemed shameful that the average family had few of the modern conveniences we enjoy in the US. Even Americans who lived inside our embassy compound occasionally dealt with bread and other perishable food shortages. US diplomatic housing was quite adequate, but when they got fresh fruit from abroad, they divided it carefully to make sure everyone's portions were equal.

There was almost nothing available to purchase on the local market unless you could pay in hard currency like the US dollar. Soviet rubles were ineffective, so even if you had a wheelbarrow full, they didn't have much purchasing power. ₽100 and ₽150 ruble notes became worthless overnight. People didn't trust banks, but if they tried to hoard paper money at home, their life savings would go up in smoke. I saw this same thing happen in Argentina in 1976, and it just devastated the populace. Families learned to purchase hard products, like bicycles, instead of trying to save cash. Then they at least owned something tangible that retained value.

7 March 1991, Thursday

Frank and I got up at 0400L and were ready to go by 0430L, so we went out front early and were surprised to find our escorts already sitting there. We immediately headed to the airport.

Along with the two military personnel driving us, we rode

with an American doctor for the recently established Children of Chernobyl Relief Fund, now called Chernobyl Children International (CCI).

Frank and I sat in the back row of the jeep, where the seats were elevated enough to prevent us from looking out the front windshield. Curtains were drawn across the side windows as well, which meant we couldn't see where we were going. Struggling to keep our backs straight to prevent spinal injury, we bounced along the very bumpy pavement for fifty minutes to Chkalovsky Air Base, just twenty-five miles to the northeast. Chkalovsky supports Star City, the center of the Soviet space program. We headed toward the famed Yuri Gagarin Cosmonaut Training Center, where Soviet cosmonauts had trained alongside US and other astronauts since 1973 for the Apollo-Soyuz Test Project. Our nations would yet cooperate in what would become the International Space Station.

During the Soviet era, this was a highly classified area. Worldwide cooperation for the space station hadn't yet materialized, so they still closely guarded the location of Star City. This mentality was evidenced by our "blindfolded" jeep ride. (I noticed in a subsequent journey in the Mriya that security loosened up substantially over the next ten months.)

After the car came to a stop, they led us into an old, unkempt building that served as the base operations center. The AN-225 had not yet arrived from its home base in Kiev, so we waited for over an hour in the flight planning room alongside the runway.

I was living a fantasy. I'd first felt the urge to visit Moscow some ten years prior, and now here I was.

Word finally came that they were ready for us. Again, we boarded the austere jeep, sat on the raised platform in the back, curtains drawn so we couldn't see out. It was the next best thing to being blindfolded. After a brief ride across the tarmac, we came to a sudden stop and they motioned for us to get out on the right. The jeep was parked very close to the port side of the forward fuselage of this monstrosity. As I stepped out, all I could make out was a large, undefinable structure. The thing was so massive that, from my up-close vantage point, I recognized no familiar lines in the shape of an airplane.

I turned to look behind me and marveled at the thirty-two wheels needed to support the million-plus pounds of cargo this mammoth could handle fully loaded! It certainly was a dream machine. The NATO designator "Cossack" didn't fit the beauty of this beast at all.

The main purpose of the impressive AN-225 had been to transport the Soviet Buran space shuttle piggyback style. Its wingspan was 68' wider than the largest US aircraft of the time, the C-5 Galaxy. It was 28' longer nose-to-tail and had a maximum gross weight of 1.3 million pounds, compared to 837,000 pounds for the Galaxy.

Bradley International Airport, Connecticut, was our

Capt. Whicker in front of the AN-225

destination. From takeoff to touchdown was 11.6 hours, according to my logbook. Frank and I slept in crew bunks for the first seven hours of the flight. We needed the sleep, and we didn't have any duties aboard the craft until approaching US airspace. We got pretty hungry though — they didn't feed us anything except apple or grape juice and crackers. Normally, they took better care of us than that, but not this time.

The airplane flew nicely. The captain's kindness shone through as he extended an invitation for me to sit in his seat, granting me a special moment during the cruise. (Of course, it was on autopilot the entire time and the copilot was sitting across from me, so there wasn't much effort involved.)

At one point during the flight, I heard a United Airlines pilot ask Boston Center over the radio, "Center, what *is* that thing at our ten o'clock position?"

"That's a Soviet Antonov 225, the world's largest airplane."

"Holy cow! That thing is HUGE!" If an airline pilot could recognize the massiveness of our plane from a mile away in a clean, no-gear configuration, you can imagine what it looked like on the ground. We had to be careful to ensure the designed capacity of runways, taxiways and parking spots was adequate for its weight.

Unfortunately, no one introduced us to the small but important entourage of passengers riding in the back. All we knew was that their purpose was to retrieve medical supplies for children who had suffered from the horrible nuclear disaster at Chernobyl five years earlier, in 1986.

Among the few passengers on this important flight was a young, bright, smiley eleven-year-old girl named Marianka Romanytch and her mother. Marianka had been diagnosed with leukemia as a result of radiation from the Chernobyl explosion when she was only six. The New Jersey-based Children of

Chernobyl Relief Fund had spent the last couple of years fundraising to provide relief to Miss Romanytch and thousands like her.

As the face of the charity, Marianka was perfect. She had a beautiful smile, was shy, and clutched a teddy bear in one hand while she clung close to her mother, Lyuba. She was the same age as my twin daughters, so I personally felt strong twinges of compassion for her.[36]

Chernobyl victim arrives — *Eleven-year-old Marianka Romanytch is mobbed after she arrives at Bradley International Airport on Thursday. Romanytch, who has leukemia, arrived in the world's largest aircraft, the Soviet-built Antonov 225.*

Such a tiny package for the world's largest airplane to deliver! She stole the show as they took her to the Yale Comprehensive Cancer Center in New Haven after we landed. Dr. Peter Beardsley, a pediatric oncologist, donated his services to treat her for at least the next year.

A large group of about one hundred fifty Ukrainian-Americans met us as we deplaned about noon Connecticut time. They greeted the captain as a hero for delivering Marianka from so far away. Even more impressive, however, was two hundred tons of medical supplies worth $300 million waiting to be loaded for the return trip. There were a bunch of record-keeping computers, ultrasound and mammogram machines, lab equipment needed for the children's care, incubators, respirators,

---

36. Later, in June 1991, we escorted an IL-62 filled with one hundred fifty children of Chernobyl who were invited to a summer camp in New England by the Samantha Smith Foundation.
https://www.samanthasmith.info/foundation

laparoscopic instruments, and, according to their spokesperson, $20,000 worth of Asparaginase and Vincristine, two important medications used to treat leukemia. All of that was going to the charity's 170-bed hospital. In addition, there were seventy-eight computers meant for technology-starved schools in Ukraine.

Weeks before, engine trouble had delayed the arrival of our big jet. It had been scheduled to come on December 28th. Now that it was here more than two months later, it was a big draw. The Soviets offered the American public $15 tickets to tour the interior of the airplane.

Frank and I caught an early flight home the next morning. A new set of Shotgunners would escort the Mriya home. It had been a wonderful trip, but I was ready to be home. My wife and children need me, and we were preparing for a new baby to arrive in just two short weeks!

As I researched for this book, I found Marianka stayed in Connecticut for the rest of her life, though I could reach no relatives to find out about her quality of life. She was born on 24 February 1980 and lived seventeen years from the time she first started treatment in the US before she passed away unexpectedly at the Yale New Haven Hospital on 3 August 2008. Her obituary[37] states she achieved a bachelor's degree in 2002 and was working on a master's at the time of her death.

With wings of steel and hope, the Mriya had carried her into the heart of a dream she would never have known.

---

37. https://tinyurl.com/ChernobylObit

18—Record-Journal, Meriden, Conn., Tuesday, March 19, 1991

Largest cargo plane flies to Ukraine

The six-engine aircraft will carry supplies to a 160-bed children's hospital built by the Children of Chernobyl Relief Fund.

WINDSOR LOCKS (AP) — The largest cargo plane in the world was loaded Monday with medical supplies for a Ukranian hospital treating victims of the Chernobyl nuclear disaster.

About 100 people, most of them Ukrainian-Americans, gathered at Bradley Airport to say farewell to the Soviet-built Antonov-225 airplane before its scheduled takeoff Tuesday. One of the well-wishers was 11-year-old Marianka Romanytch, a leukemia victim who was transported to Connecticut for treatment in the giant aircraft almost two weeks ago.

The child's mother, Lyoba Romanytch, said the plane's 150 tons of supplies are desperately needed in her home country.

"They're waiting. There's absolutely nothing to treat them with there," said Lyoba Romanytch, the girl's mother.

Romanytch, who lived about 20 miles from the Chernobyl plant at the time of the 1986 accident, was diagnosed with leukemia less than a year ago. She has been undergoing treatment at Yale-New Haven Hospital.

The crowd sang the Ukranian national anthem and participated in a brief prayer service amid the boxes of supplies already loaded in the cavernous aircraft. A group of children from St. Michael's Ukranian School in Hartford, wearing traditional Ukranian folk costumes, presented the pilot with a bouquet of flowers.

"Please carry our greetings to the children of the Ukraine," said one gaily dressed girl, a wreath of flowers adorning her hair.

The six-engine aircraft will carry supplies to a 160-bed children's hospital built by the Children of Chernobyl Relief Fund, a Short Hills, N.J.-based agency aimed at helping victims of the disaster.

Among the items on board will be computers for hospital record-keeping, equipment to perform ultrasounds and mammograms, laboratory equipment, incubators, respirators and laproscopic equipment, said Zenon Matkiwsky, president of the Fund.

The Fund bought most of the equipment at discounted prices, while some of it was donated, Matkiwsky said.

Also on board will be a variety of medicines, including $20,000 worth of Asparginase and Vincrystine, two medications for the treatment of leukemia that are unavailable in the Soviet Union, he said.

The two medications will treat 20 children for 28 days, said Matkiwsky's wife, Nadia. There are 70 leukemia patients already at the hospital, she said.

The aircraft is also being used to transport 78 computers that will be donated to schools in the Ukraine.

Zenon Matkiwsky said he will travel to the Soviet Union in April to investigate the possibility of opening a second hospital.

Chapter 14 - Coup d'état

пути не будет
"There will be no way"

29 August 1991, Thursday

"We all hoped we'd have the opportunity to perform this year," Yuri Ermakov, part of a thirty-person delegation from the Soviet Ministry of Civil Aviation, expressed in his best English. His feelings probably ran much deeper than the news reporters even realized; the 1991 MiG-29 Friendship Tour almost didn't happen at all.

This long-anticipated junket was set to create international goodwill and develop business contacts in America as Gorbachev's *perestroika* initiative led the Soviet Union toward a more capitalistic stance.

Mr. Ermakov punctuated his arrival statement with an air of relief: "We're glad to finally be here." Behind that simple expression was a long, convoluted story that began ten days prior...

18 August 1991, Sunday

"Lisbeth," I whispered into the phone to my wife's best friend, who lived a few blocks from us.

"Oh, hi! Just a minute, I'll get John," Lisbeth said, chopping something in the background in preparation for Sunday dinner.

"No, actually, I wanted to talk to you. I have to leave right after church today to go meet some Russians in Alaska."

"So soon after Pam's surgery? How's she doing?"

"She seems to be doing okay, but I worry about her — a lot. Would you keep an extra close eye on her this week?"

"Absolutely. Of course," she replied energetically. Lisbeth was the leader of our church's local women's organization, and she took that role seriously, sagaciously filling the needs of the women she oversaw.

"I should be back by Thursday at the latest."

"No problem at all. We're here to help."

"You're amazing, Lisbeth! Thank you so much!"

I hung up, satisfied that things were in order for my departure. It was nice to have such good people surrounding us. I never had to worry about leaving the family alone. I was confident my wife and five daughters, now including a newborn, would be well cared for.

We gathered our whole gaggle, each of the girls smartly dressed with their hair perfectly coiffed. Their mother was fastidious about making sure they always looked sharp.

As we piled into our eight-passenger van and headed to church, none of us had any inkling of the momentous events taking place elsewhere. News outlets wouldn't even get wind of the transformative drama unfolding halfway across the world until later that night.

President Mikhail Gorbachev was at that very hour being threatened by the so-called "Gang of Eight" while relaxing at his vacation dacha in the Crimea. Officially dubbed the State Committee on the State of Emergency, or GKChP in Russian, the group declared Gennady Yanayev, the country's second in command, as acting USSR president because of Gorbachev's "inability to perform presidential duties due to illness."

There was no illness. These men were merely unhappy with their president's restructuring efforts under *perestroika* and were determined to put a stop to them by pronouncing Mr. Gorbachev unfit.

Despite Lisbeth's assurances, I dreaded having to leave my my wife, who was still recovering from a difficult birth four months before.

"I'm sorry I have to go again, Pam. This job has sure become much busier than I anticipated. Will you and the girls be okay?"

I knew her answer before she voiced it: She would plow forward, no matter how hard the circumstances. I'd always compared my wife to a pioneer woman — beautiful and sensitive, but tough to the bone. Even while we were dating, I got the sense that she could power through any trial.

She had strong faith and a determination to be the best mother on the planet. She was basically raising our five daughters on her own, and even though I was climbing the career ladder and providing a comfortable home and food on the table, I always felt a little guilty about my frequent absences. Our twins, Cami and Tara, were eleven years old now. There was some comfort in knowing they were such great little helpers.

I rushed to the airport, and after an uneventful but very long flight, I arrived in Anchorage in the early evening hours, ready to meet the Soviets coming in the next day for their much-ballyhooed MiG-29 Friendship Tour. A fellow Shotgunner, Tom, picked me up at the airport, and we went straight to the Elmendorf AFB billeting office to get rooms for the night.

As I got ready for bed, I absently switched on the TV and was stunned into full wakefulness as reports of the terrible constitutional crisis trickled in. Minimal details became clearer over the next hour. The world's news machines were ablaze with word that political rivals had ousted Mikhail Gorbachev from power while he rested near the Black Sea.

Within the last year, I had graduated with a master's degree in international relations, with an emphasis on Soviet studies, from the University of Southern California's overseas program. Along with the rest of the free world, the unique and timely changes being made in the USSR enthralled me. Gorbachev's reforms had already altered the structure of his government, elevating his title from General Secretary and Chairman of the Supreme Soviet to President in 1990. Now it was becoming obvious that his *glasnost* and *perestroika* policies were not as popular among his political peers as they were in the West.

Sitting on the edge of the bed, I was mesmerized by the commentator's analysis of the evolving upheaval. I buried my head in my hands and said a brief prayer, hoping against hope that this takeover would fail. I desperately wanted the USSR to emerge from its outdated ways to become the promising democracy I'd foreseen as I studied Gorbachev's bold new initiatives.

The coup attempt on his presidency was underway just as the participating MiGs and their accompanying support aircraft, the IL-76 Candid, unwittingly punched through the airways across the frozen Siberian tundra en route to the first of seven American air shows planned for their tour.

19 August 1991, Monday

In his acclaimed book from 2001, *Aerozel-2*, Soviet pilot

Alexander Garnaev spoke of his experience on this day. One of two MiG-29 civilian test pilots slated to fly the non-combat-ready Fulcrums in this widely anticipated series of US air demonstrations, Garnaev was even then a renowned and decorated pilot in his motherland. Some years later, he would receive the title Hero of the Russian Federation.

"The main surprise awaited us in Alaska," he wrote in his book. And what a surprise it was! At 7 a.m. Monday morning, I fielded a call from Washington, DC, saying that the US State Department had rescinded their previously issued diplomatic clearance for this Soviet entourage and we were to turn them back immediately.

"*You've got to be kidding me*," I thought, nervously twirling the hotel phone cord around my finger. I was thinking what a goat-rope this would be — me, a measly Captain in the Air Force, having to tell a forty-man foreign contingent, who were supposed to be honored guests, to go home! How would they take the news?

Of course, I couldn't argue with the guy on the other end of the phone. He was just another lowly messenger. The decision had been made at many levels of authority above any of us.

I fretted, wondering if the incoming pilots had any inkling of what was happening back in their country. They'd already been traveling for a couple of days by now. Crossing Siberia on their way to Alaska was no small feat, I knew.

At 12:00 noon sharp, the two visiting MiGs touched down smoothly at the base's two-mile-long runway. It was a joy to watch them approach and land. They were gorgeous aircraft I'd only ever seen in pictures. It struck me that these were the enemy I had trained to fight, but now, I was about to eagerly shake the pilots' hands in friendship ... and then refuse them entry.

My dread at having to relay the bad news was relieved by the sudden appearance of the Lieutenant General in Command of the 11th Air Force and NORAD's[38] Alaskan Region. Wearing his impressive three stars, he arrived at Base Ops just in time to meet the delegation. As the ranking officer at Elmendorf, he was a much more appropriate and believable conveyor of the grim reality that faced these unsuspecting guests.

They were all escorted into the Distinguished Visitors Lounge, where we learned the group had some notion of the developing coup back home. A small transistor radio carried by one of the pilots had captured small bits of news at one of their refueling stops. Still, the official message from our State department telling them not to continue on to Anchorage had not reached them before they took off from Anadyr on the east coast of the USSR that morning.

"Because of the upheaval created by the coup, the US Secretary of State has unfortunately had to withdraw your diplomatic clearance to enter the mainland," the General gently told the head of the delegation, somewhat chagrined himself. One of the immutable tenets of the American system was civilian rule. Even a star-studded General had no choice but to follow the orders of appointed government officials.

The look of disbelief on the faces of our Soviet friends was unmistakable as their mouths dropped open and their shoulders stooped with the weight of the communique. It was

---

38. North American Aerospace Defense Command, established in 1958, is a joint US-Canadian command responsible for aerospace warning, aerospace control, and maritime warning for Canada, Alaska, and the continental United States. https://sgp.fas.org/crs/natsec/R42077.pdf p. 42.

as if the entire world had caved in on them. The Friendship Tour had been in the works for a long time.

"After refueling, you'll have to turn around and fly back home."

The message was hard to take, not only for the occupants of the three Soviet jets who had just made a 3,800-nautical-mile trip through severe and even dangerous weather conditions, but also for us as their American hosts. Everyone seemed to move slowly. The figurative wind had been blown out of all our sails. One of the female officers from the USAF protocol office even had tears in her eyes.

We scrambled to find something we could do for these new friends who had traveled so far. Personally, I felt embarrassed to reject them, even though I partially understood the larger implications. The MiG-29 had been seen in European shows, but this was supposed to be its first appearance at US venues. Americans felt a magnetic draw to witness a rare enemy MiG-29 Fulcrum perform its full repertoire of aeronautical feats and I hated to see our country miss out on the opportunity.

Gorbachev had gained popularity among most Russians, and this small visiting group expressed concern that his reformations would now be abruptly halted. More than that, they were worried about their own families. Lawless rioting and unrest was being reported in the streets of Moscow on the overhead television.

"Do you think this is the end for Gorbachev?" I asked Alexander Garnaev, who was one of the MiG pilots.

He shook his head, "*Ne znayu*. I don't know what to expect," he replied, "but it's all nonsense. I bet this Gang of Eight attempt will not last more than ten days."

He didn't like the unexpected interruption any more than we did. The eight Soviet conspirators, by their self-serving action, had destabilized not only this historic air show tour, but multiple delicate and important negotiations underway elsewhere:

- Soviet government officials were at that moment offering critical assistance to achieve the release of American and Western European hostages kidnapped by Hezbollah aficionados during the Lebanon Hostage Crisis.

- Gorbachev and President George H. W. Bush had signed START I, the original Strategic Arms Reduction Treaty, less than three weeks before, and the capricious state of the USSR leadership could now jeopardize it.

- The withdrawal of 45,000 Soviet troops from Poland had begun in April. Would this turbulence also disrupt that important demobilization?

"I hope my wife and kids are safe," Alexander whispered under his breath. Being a family man myself, I fully understood his concern.

I helped him and a few others place phone calls to connect with loved ones to ascertain their safety amid this chaos. That act alone solidified our friendship.

Alexander was especially grateful when he got through to his wife, Allyona. He could only talk for a couple of minutes, but as he hung up, he told me she seemed to be okay and reported that the *putschists* had taken control of the newspapers and radio stations in Moscow.

"We aren't getting a clear picture of what's going on. All I can tell you is there are riots and unrest all around. But she and our children, Masha and Youri, are safe."

The base fed the entire group at the Officer's Club, and we had plenty of opportunity to talk while the planes were refueled.

"Alexander," one of our intelligence officers said, pulling up a chair and nudging the MiG pilot. "You know, with all this turmoil in your country, you have the right under international law to exercise the option to stay and request political asylum in the United States."

Dumbfounded, Alexander glanced furtively toward the KGB officer at the adjoining table. The group had nicknamed him "Grandfather-U," though I never understood the rationale behind that moniker.

"Ummm ... that's a kind offer, but I have a family at home and need to get back to them to make sure they're okay."

"That's understandable," replied our guy. "I just wanted you to know it was on the table." And with that, he stepped away. There was no effort to persuade.

Not one of them accepted the offer. Perhaps it was made in too-obvious earshot of Grandfather-U, but more likely, it was a sense of pride in their country and ties to family and friends that prevented them from severing their lifelong connections. In general, individuals plan and premeditate political defections well in advance. I don't think there was serious thought that any would accept the invitation on such a hasty timeline.

The only way forward was to return to Moscow to see what their future held.

Chapter 15 - Reversal

Раз на раз не приходится
"From time to time, it does not happen"

19 August 1991, Monday (continued)

Alexander Garnaev, Hero of the USSR

Alexander was especially friendly to Tom and I. He even let us sit in the cockpit of the MiG-29 "Fulcrum" — quite a thrill! There were obvious distinctions between this Soviet-made aircraft and our fighter jets, but it was clear this was a fine flying machine. While the American F-15C "Eagle" was faster, had a higher service ceiling and quadruple the range, the MiG was slightly smaller and lighter and thus reportedly more maneuverable and could easily out-climb the Eagle in feet per minute.

I will always maintain that our aircraft are better built than their Soviet counterparts, but any new experience in any airplane was intoxicating! If only we could talk these neoteric friends into an orientation flight in the two-seater model! Unfortunately, such an opportunity never materialized. We took several photos of Tom and me in the cockpit, but I cannot locate them.

It was a 900-nautical-mile trip back to Anadyr in the Soviet Far East, so crew rest considerations ruled out any lingering. Besides, the Soviets were anxious to return to their families and try to make sense of the catastrophe drastically transforming their world.

Still, refueling delays held them over much longer than the

proposed ninety-minute turnaround. When I saw they would be with us another hour or more, I approached Alexander.

"I'd like to send you home with a token of our friendship. You have two children, yes? What is something they would want from America?"

"Oh, Glenn! They have dreamed of owning a Walkman. But that would be hard to get on short notice. How expensive are they?"

"I don't know, but I'll be right back." I was eager to make their trip worthwhile, and Alexander and I had hit it off so well that I thought this could do the trick. Normally, we would have given them a chance to shop for themselves at our Base Exchange (BX), but circumstances didn't allow it.

I rushed over to the BX, purchased a Walkman tape player for about $40, and ran back to Base Ops. Alexander was already strapping into his jet by the time I returned. I ran onto the ramp, climbed the stubby ladder hooked over the cockpit edge, and leaned over the canopy rail.

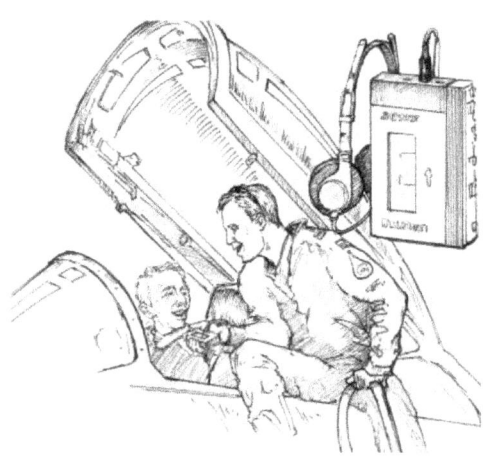

"Please give this to Youri," I said as I presented the small package. "Tell him I hope to meet him someday."

It's doubtful, but I thought I saw the beginnings of a tear form in this tough fighter pilot's eye. "*Spasibo*," he gratefully replied, as his outstretched arm planted a powerful slap of friendship squarely on my shoulder. "He will be thrilled."

And with that, he turned his full attention to the detailed

preflight checklist for the long flight home. I jumped down to get out of the way, knowing very well the level of concentration needed to handle such a complicated machine safely. I could only hope that we'd have the chance to meet again someday.

20 to 22 August 1991, Tuesday - Thursday

I sat exhausted, sullen, and defeated, reclined in my economy seat of a Delta jet on my way back from Anchorage to Mainland USA. I know there were many others, notably the Soviet pilots and crew chiefs, who were even more disappointed. All had worked so hard to make this an event to remember, and it had been a total bust.

On the bright side, waiting at home was my gorgeous wife and five beautiful daughters, including baby Lyndsey, born in Virginia just four months ago. Night had fallen by the time I made my way to our cozy little house. I gently opened the front door, the house dark and quiet, and as I passed the bedroom of my sleeping pre-teen twins, I could hear the heavy breathing of slumber that announced all was well. Catching sight of an older tape player sitting on their bedside table, I thought of the little Russian boy who would soon place his own cherished Walkman near his head as he climbed into bed. I hoped for a future where such shared experiences would outweigh the differences that separated our worlds today.

I had bonded especially well with baby Lyndsey since her mother had been so sick for the first several months of her life. I was lucky to still have a wife. Infection had plagued Pam after the baby's birth. While she lay recovering in the hospital, I spent many sleepless nights rocking and walking our newborn at home, trying to calm her from the colic she suffered much of the time.

By the Thursday after my return, I was again fully engrossed in professional matters when news sources began to hint that the big, bad coup in the USSR had already ended! My heart felt lighter because not only could we resurrect the Friendship Tour, but a considerably brighter future loomed for a magnificent country that had long been oppressed by its own government.

The openness and restructuring promised by Mr. Gorbachev were once again free to be implemented. The military had not thrown their full weight behind the Gang of Eight, forcing the conspirators to back down from their lofty plan to derail the innovations of *perestroika*. They had despised such unprecedented changes and were particularly against a proposed union treaty that would decentralize Soviet-style government power and distribute it to the individual republics.

In the end, Gorbachev's fresh, more democratic concepts prevailed. It was almost like a brand-new nation was materializing. Now that the crisis was over, the hoped-for progress could gain more momentum than if the coup had never taken place.

Ironically, however, it proved to be the beginning of the end for President Gorbachev himself. By Christmas, he would step down with a peaceful and voluntary resignation instead of being forced out by increasingly hard-core innovators. Boris Yeltsin, a figurehead who thought Gorbachev's reforms were too slow, was quickly gaining favor.

23 August 1991, Friday

I scrambled all day, trying to piece together all of the unraveled components of a complicated international air extravaganza. There were heavy governmental hurdles to overcome in short order. The Cleveland National Air Show, the first of six scheduled stops remaining on the Friendship Tour, was to kick off in just one week. It was already too late to salvage the planned Westfield Massachusetts appearance because of the coup's interference with the timeline.

The USSR's political troubles had trickled down into the dynamics of my very busy family life, requiring duplication of time and effort on the same trip we'd already accomplished once! Thankfully, my partner, Captain Brian Green, stayed right with me as we juggled two or three simultaneous phone calls each throughout the entire workday. Sometimes I addressed him by his formal name, but mostly, it was just 'Greenie.' I never asked him if he was okay with that nickname, but everyone called me 'Whick' without my input.

Finally, we had it all sorted, with me on track to go up to Anchorage the next morning to once again greet the Soviet flyers.

"Glenn," Pam reminded me as I explained the plan later that evening. "Don't you remember? We are getting our family portrait done tomorrow!"

Oh, boy! I boofed that. There was nothing more important to me than my role as husband and dad. I couldn't let a simple international incident keep me from my number one priority! I made a last tweak to the renewed arrangements we'd hammered out and decided I'd hustle up to Alaska on Sunday instead, barely in time to greet the returning contingent the next morning.

I provided much of the baby's care when I was home to give my wife a chance to rest and heal. Things were stressful, to say the least. It didn't help that I had lost Pam's wedding ring after she gave it to me for safekeeping before she went into surgery to deliver. Too small for any but my pinky finger, I fell asleep while waiting for her to come out of recovery. When I walked across the hospital lawn that night to go home, I forgot about the ring until I got to the car. When I realized it was gone, I retraced my steps several times, desperately looking for it.

It was never found.

I had to admit to her that I lost it while she was still suffering from her C-section. A few days before this repeat trip, I was finally able to afford a new ring, four months after the loss. I couldn't very well miss family pictures too!

Part of my job on these missions was to ensure foreign pilots carried current airway and instrument charts for every possible destination airfield. These were long before the days of the electronic flight bags (EFB). In 1991, pilots had to lug around dozens of booklets containing the information required to land safely anywhere, under any weather conditions. The paper maps were heavy and conveyed by hand in a hard leather briefcase. My dad, a professional flight engineer for his forty-year flying career, ruined his back and wrists from carrying around fifty-pound pub bags until those fancy little carts with wheels came along. Then he got smart and just pulled trolleys containing his stacks of books. Today, everything a pilot needs to navigate fits in a lightweight iPad. You can access air publications that cover the entire world in one hand, and they are continuously updated wirelessly.

My dad's flight pub bag

But in 1991, everything was still on paper, and as I rushed around in preparation for the renewed Friendship Tour, I stopped by Base Operations to procure the latest editions of these important publications covering our flight path. I also had to double-check that the FAA-approved routing hadn't changed since last week. Their international office coordinated with the State Department to ensure all Soviet flights kept clear of confidential areas. Luckily, for this event, I didn't have to go to the Soviet Embassy in Washington, DC, for a visa to enter their country. For this trip, they were given special dispensation to fly as far as Anchorage without an escort and would already be inside US airspace by the time we got on board — one less item to complete.

24 August 1991, Saturday

Freeing up my schedule on Saturday allowed me some much-needed time with family. My older three daughters had agreed to substitute for a neighbor girl's paper route, so I took them to deliver papers at 6:45 a.m. Then we went straight over to mow the church lawn. No one had touched it in a couple of weeks, and it was in dire need of some loving attention. Then it was on to the promised photo pose. In case it never crossed your mind, family portraits get more complicated the more children you have. Our Saturday picture-taking session turned out to be quite the comedy of errors! But we managed it, and the resulting portrait was quite pleasant.

After a brief rest, Pam and I broke away for a date with friends. We enjoyed an excellent dinner at the Outback Steakhouse, then excused ourselves momentarily to come home to change Pam's wound dressing, as she was experiencing some discomfort. It was lucky we came home when we did, because our twins, age eleven, were struggling with four-month-old Lyndsey. She was teething and had been screaming for quite a while. The girls didn't know what to do. As soon as the baby saw me, she cried harder and reached out to me with a trembling arm, as if to say, "Save me, Daddy!" I held her tight and fed her a little, and she went right to sleep. All she craved was the reassurance of security in the arms of a parent.

Flight Pubs

Paper flight publications are a thing of the past in today's digital world. Instead of lugging around a sixty-pound locking leather briefcase stuffed with current maps, charts, and references needed to execute a cross-country flight, pilots now carry small hand-held tablets. Electronic Flight Bags (EFBs) are mini marvels where aircrews can pull up unlimited navigational charts, screens with visual depictions of current weather threats, temporary flight restrictions (TFRs), Notices to Airmen (NOTAMs), advisories and service bulletins.

Flight-related data is in constant flux. Airways, radio frequencies, airspace designations, and even airport names are frequently updated to reflect changes to obstacles, airfield construction, and no-fly zones. Not familiar with your destination? Instantly pull up its airport diagram. Got a sudden crisis on your hands? Open the emergency checklist for your situation by the touch of a finger.

Printed versions of these required publications expire every couple of months. In my day, we had to swap out books and charts every few weeks to ensure we had the latest data onboard. That took time and effort. By transforming all such references to weightless electrons, thousands of tiny changes can be updated instantly by the click of a mouse.

Tech Tab #4

Enhanced safety is only one of the great advantages gained by this new technology: a pilot's ability to digest mountains of information is bolstered. Complicated info that was once conveyed verbally is now represented visually and in color! Critical items such as a change to a landing procedure or a traffic pattern altitude can be updated instantly, rather than having to wait for the next printing. Serious accidents have occurred due to ignorance of changes at a destination airport.

"Pubs" as we called them, also include conversion charts, descriptions of Special Use Airspace (SUA), aircraft performance tables, etc. For example, you cannot just fly willy-nilly over the Grand Canyon; there are specific ground tracks and altitudes you must follow if you don't want to have your license revoked. Manuals specific to your aircraft, weight and balance calculators, and performance charts can also be made accessible on these devices.

An EFB is an all-purpose, living personalized library.

25 August 1991, Sunday

5:00 a.m. came awfully early. A taxi arrived on time at 0545 hours to get me to Dulles International Airport. With a long layover in Salt Lake City, where my mom lived, I squeezed in a visit with her before finally landing in Anchorage late that night.

Tomorrow would start our *déjà vu* experience.

Chapter 16 - Reborn

Лучше поздно, чем никогда
"Better late than never"

26 August 1991, Monday

Jon, my partner on this trip, met me over breakfast at 0830L. This was his first Shotgun gig, so I wanted to prepare him. We briefed the day's three-legged mission: Anchorage to Juneau (PAED[39]-PAJN), 500 nautical miles (nm);[40] Juneau to Minot AFB, North Dakota (PAJN-KMOT), 1,300 nm; and finally, Minot to Burke Field in Cleveland (KMOT-KBKL), another 925 nm.

"Why are we only going 500 miles on this first leg?" Jon asked with a twinkle in his eye.

"Because it's a goodwill gesture," I answered. "There are important people in the capital city of Alaska who want to see these 'enemy' jets and get a better feel for the monumental changes happening in the Soviet Union. It'll just be a short stop, and then we'll be on our way."

We also wanted our flying comrades to experience this gorgeous part of the United States. Settled between Mt. Juneau and Mt. Roberts, Alaska's capital has a beauty all its own. Trees meet sparkling water and wide, miles-long glaciers. Row after row of mountains stretch to the horizon, reflected in the water of lakes dyed a bluish hue by the silt of melting ice and snow.

---

39. Every airport in the world has a four-letter identifier. The letter "P" precedes all Alaskan and Hawaiian airports (for Pacific), "C" all Canadian, and "K" all "K"ontinental US airports.
40. A nautical mile is about 1.15 statute miles.

Braided rivers find circuitous routes, meandering through valleys shaped eons ago by slow-moving glaciers.

Jon and I would fly in the IL-76 transport plane, in full radio contact with the MiGs in loose formation close by.

"Hey, do you think they'd allow one of us to fly the short leg to Juneau in the back seat of the UB[41] trainer?" Jon asked. The thought hadn't crossed my mind, but of course, what a great idea!

Each of the two MiGs on this trip was a different model. How I would have loved to hitch a ride in one of those glamorous jets, even for just one hop! But I wasn't bold enough to ask, thinking the ice hadn't yet thawed adequately between our Cold War superpowers to allow such a thing.

So I told Jon no. Afterward, I wished I'd pursued the opportunity when we discovered that the Soviets were offering twenty-minute rides in the two-seater for a cool $10,000! I also didn't know then that a Canadian F-18 pilot[42] had flown a MiG-29 at the Canadian Abbottsford Air Show two years before. Maybe they would have let us take a back seat!

We reported to Elmendorf's base operations at 1100L, exactly one hour prior to the two MiGs' landing at noon. Their arrival was spectacular, as usual, and we were glad to see the Friendship Tour back on track. The accompanying IL-76 arrived thirty minutes later. We met the crews on the ramp of the flight line.

Alexander was the first to greet me, this time with a big bear hug. "Youri loves the Walkman you sent home. It was a huge surprise to him. Thanks again!"

---

41. Учебно-Боевой: "UB" is the designation for the two-seat combat trainer version of a Soviet aircraft. The front seat is for the student, and the rear is for the instructor.

42. https://coldwarconversations.com/episode106/

OHIO
Jet rides available – for $10,000

Soviet MiGs at air show

CLEVELAND (AP) — Soviet pilots delayed by the coup in Moscow have arrived for this weekend's Cleveland National Air Show with an intriguing offer — MiG-29 rides for $10,000.

Two MiG pilots were part of a 30-member Soviet delegation that arrived aboard two MiG-29's and an IL-76 cargo plane Wednesday.

Pilots will perform at the Cleveland show, then head to Westfield, Mass., Mankato, Minn., Harrisburg, Pa., Topeka, Kan., Fort Worth, Texas, and Salinas, Calif., to perform in air shows over the next few weeks.

Rides aboard the MiG-29 will be sold for $10,000, but there are more people interested in flying than available flight time, Cleveland air show executive director Chuck Newcomb said.

These guys had flown across eight time zones to get home, spent two nights with their families, and then turned right around to do it all again. Three one-way trips in ten days, for a grand total of well over 13,000 statute miles. That's the equivalent of going from New York to Los Angeles four and a half times! For the two MiG pilots, all those miles were endured in a cramped fighter cockpit where you can't get up to grab a cup of coffee or use the bathroom. We had to admire their tenacity.

"What do you think about the coup attempt?" I asked.

"I knew it wouldn't last long," Alexander confidently asserted. "I even made a bet with Valera (the Ilyushin navigator), "that it would fail within ten days."

Even so, it had been important for the crew members to get "eyes on" their families to know they were safe during all the civic turmoil. Alexander had taken time with his wife to visit the Russian White House[43] on the newly named Free Russia Square. He personally saw the barricades around that symbolic political icon and listened to many of the emotional speeches delivered in the town center.

To a person, the entire entourage seemed to approve of the positive way things turned out for Gorby.

"Gorbachev will remain in control, but with reduced responsibilities," Alexander conjectured. Evidently, the coup had produced a satisfactory compromise that almost everyone could live with, including greater power of autonomy for each of the separate republics.

The refueling of the planes went smoothly, and as we were getting ready to walk across the tarmac to board the airplanes, our friendly three-star General showed up out of nowhere, just as he had the week before, this time bearing a whole new bombshell.

"Glenn, I can't let you go to Juneau."

What? Talk about a shock! Specific routing for this journey to the Ohio Air Show had already gone through the FAA, the State Department, and the Pentagon. Everyone in authority had approved it. The General's F-15s from NORAD were going to accompany us halfway on this first leg, then turn around to land back at Elmendorf. Two F-16s were sitting alert on the ramp at Juneau even now, ready to launch in time to meet us at the hand-off point where the F-15s pulled out. It was all well-orchestrated

---

43. Two years later, Captain Chuck Miller and I stood on the bridge across from this administrative building and watched it burn as yet another Russian crisis unfolded.

and fully authorized by the highest powers. The weather was flawless, the arrival runway was plenty long, and there was a safe, published instrument approach to the city's airport that made navigation between the extraordinarily high surrounding mountains perfectly safe. Why was the General inserting himself into the design, suddenly prohibiting a landing at Juneau?

True, from a pilot's perspective, Juneau's unique terrain presents some issues. It's the nation's isolated state capital in that it is only accessible by boat or plane. To the east is a range of mountains that rise to about 10,000 feet along a narrow canal. Because of terrain limitations, there is no "straight-in" instrument approach to the airfield. The final approach course is 069°, but the runway is oriented to 080°, so you always end up two miles out pointed more than 10 degrees off runway heading. In the "soup," such geometry can make for some challenging landings, but the weather was perfectly good today.

As anyone with military experience understands, a mere Air Force Captain like me could hardly stand up to a three-star General. Even so, I was peeved enough that I had to say something!

"Sir," I interjected, getting up my nerve. "This is a flight of international significance, approved by multiple government agencies, and it has diplomatic status. We can't just change things up for no good reason."

He sensed the utter dismay in my voice.

"You need to go through Comox Valley Airport instead," he calmly commanded, never revealing his reasoning. There was no option left but to obey a superior officer. I could only guess what was behind the demand.

Two years prior, in July 1989, the 11th Air Force had provided gateway host services for a similar air tour of MiGs that performed at Abbottsford, British Columbia. As the head of the

Alaskan NORAD Region, it may be that the General felt he owed an international crony at Comox Canadian Forces Base (CFB) a favor by allowing him to get in on the action this time around. Or perhaps there was something going on in Juneau that week to which I was not privy. In any case, his requirement was certainly making, and would yet make, this whole project more difficult.[44]

Jon and I spent much of that day working on a revised flight clearance to Comox. This wasn't just the standard planning process. It had suddenly turned from a domestic to an international flight plan, meaning we had to coordinate with all three agencies who had already cleared the previous path *plus* get Canadian approval.

And sure enough, by this one man's word, the entire Canadian government and military was made to jump through hoops to make it all work.

The kerfuffle caused us to spend an extra night in Anchorage, adding more delay to this downright ill-bred tour. Coordination and execution of these flights was not easy from the get-go, and this type of meddling was extremely frustrating.

27 August 1991, Tuesday

We finally got out of Anchorage a full day late and made the three-hour flight to Comox, a beautiful base on Vancouver Island. How big a blunder this sudden change of route would prove to be! The days ahead would be full of botched episodes.

Evidently, the commercial Fixed Base Operator (FBO) at

---

44. In subsequent years, it became obvious to the entire world that this General was very opinionated when he served as a military commentator on Fox News.

Comox was not at all happy to see us.

"They won't take your credit here, Alexander," I woefully explained.

"Why?"

"Because when your buddies came through two years ago, they left the FBO in the lurch — the credit cards defaulted." During the premier visit of the MiGs to Canada two years before, the Soviets had used American Express credit cards for their Avgas (aviation gasoline). Long after they had returned to their homeland, the Canucks found out that their credit was worthless, and the Canadian government ended up paying thousands of dollars for fuel used by their guests.

This go-round, Comox flatly refused to refuel the MiGs. Another seemingly insurmountable hurdle. What to do? It was my job as escort to ensure these guys got all the services needed to make a successful trip to Cleveland, Ohio. Now, we weren't even in the United States. I had no authority, ability, or resources to draw upon here. The pilots' expenses would be paid for by the promoters once the air demonstrations themselves were underway, but the deal was that they had to pay their own way to the starting location. We were stuck on the West Coast of British Columbia with no means of getting fuel.

Alexander relayed the bad news to the rest of the contingent. Shortly, he returned. "We have a solution," he said. "In the barren wastelands of our vast country, we often have to do this."

And then, before my incredulous eyes, I watched as the Soviet crew chiefs drug out a long, heavy hose from the cargo compartment of their support aircraft. Not to be stopped by a mere lack of money, they improvised and refueled the fighter jets from the fuel stores of the IL-76 that accompanied them, stringing the hose from the midsection of the IL-76 engine to the fuel tanks of each MiG.

In-flight air-to-air refueling was common in both the Soviet Union and the United States, so the concept of a larger aircraft acting as a fuel tanker to feed a fighter was not unusual. I'd just never seen it done on the ground, and it took some clever improvisation to make it happen.

The process was complex and the set-up wasn't perfectly suited for the job, judging by the inefficiencies I observed. They strung a hose from the midsection of one of the IL-76 engines to the fuel tanks of the MiGs. All in all, it took three full hours to accomplish a job that would have normally taken forty minutes.

The question rolled over in my mind: *What will they do at the next en-route stop when the IL-76 has no more fuel to offer? How will they pay for it?* Hopefully, this year's credit cards were backed by real money and would be accepted in the US! Things had to get easier from this point. Didn't they?

Finally, we were airborne again. Destination: Minot AFB, North Dakota.[45] At 48° 25' minutes north latitude, it is the northernmost Air Force Base in the continental US, even farther north than Loring, Maine, or Great Falls, Montana.

Almost as soon as we lifted off, ATC notified us that he wasn't receiving accurate speed, altitude, or location information. Our transponder wasn't working. That meant he couldn't provide adequate traffic separation from other aircraft, diminishing the safety factor for everyone in flight around us.

"Aeroflot 387, this is Comox Terminal Departure Control.

---

45. A common joke amongst airmen in the USAF starts by playfully asking, "Why not My-Not (Minot)?" The not-so-innocent answer to the above question is: "Freezin's the reason!" No one wants to live and work in Minot because of how blasted cold it is.

We're not receiving your radar target. Please recycle your transponder and squawk[46] 4387."

"Rawjer, Vancouver, recycling transponder. Squawking 4387."

We continued our climb, hoping that by rebooting the transponder, our in-flight status relay would start working and all would be well. Knowing the prevalence of maintenance problems encountered on any aircraft and the increased probability of such on a Soviet flight, I wasn't hopeful that such a simple remedy would do the trick.

Just as we approached the departure intersection where we could turn on a more direct course toward our destination, Comox called again:

"Ummm, Aeroflot 387, still not receiving a target. We're going to have to turn you back."

Turn us back? To the very airport that had refused to service our aircraft? I was desperate. This mission had already been delayed more than a week. We'd endured a significant change of plans, and this guy was saying we couldn't proceed. How frustrating! I got on the radio.

"Comox, this is Aeroflot 387. I'm the US Air Force escort on board, and we really need to make our destination today. We have US State Department diplomatic status. Any way you could live with a primary radar target for this one flight and let them have the transponder looked at upon arrival Minot?"

There was no delay in his response.

"Negative, Aeroflot 387. As you know, a working transponder is required to enter the PCA.[47] You'll have to turn

---

46. See Tech Tab regarding transponders, found at the end of this chapter.
47. Positive Control Airspace - the predecessor to Class A, which would be implemented in September 1993. It included any airspace above 18,000' MSL and below 60,000' MSL.

back now and get that thing fixed."

I believe, depending on the particular controller, that we could have gotten away with an inoperative transponder for just one leg in the United States in the 1990s. But this guy was playing hardball, and he wasn't going to listen to a US Air Force Captain trying to massage the rules.

"Rawjer. Aeroflot 387 turning back now."

Surely the ground personnel at Comox would be as unexcited to see us as we were to face them again.

The Soviet crew needed no interpretation. They'd entertained a sparkle of hope when I'd jumped in to run interference for them on the radio — *"Maybe this American can talk some sense into the controller,"* they were thinking—but after our latest interchange over the airwaves, you could see by their faces that they were as deflated as I was. None of us were happy campers, but what could we do? Turn back we must. Besides being bound by the rules of ICAO[48], it was the safest thing to do. The Big Sky Theory[49] generally works well, but there was no need to test it when our flight was so high profile, newsworthy, and charged with political overtones.

Back on the ground at Comox, our onboard technicians spent another two and a half hours trying to isolate the problem. They had no spare transponder with them, so their only option was to finagle the existing box that transformed the magic

---

48. International Civil Aviation Organization, the worldwide equivalent to the FAA (Federal Aviation Administration) in the US.
49. The notion that airplanes are small enough when compared to the gigantic atmosphere they're flying in as to make it improbable that two aircraft will want to occupy the same piece of air at the same time.

electrons into a reliable radar signal.

By now, the two air show coordinators onboard were a bundle of nerves. Jim and Flip had promoted this tour for several months and were there to keep tabs on things for the overall organizers. The MiGs, with their working transponders, had gone on to Minot, a couple of F-18s escorting them the rest of the way. Separating the support plane from the fighters was far from ideal.

By the time the mechanics got things squared away, it was too late to make it all the way to Ohio that day. Flip and Jim made hotel arrangements at Minot for everyone, another unanticipated expense. As I learned time and again on this job, schedule slips and cost overruns were a given when working with the Soviets.

As we later descended into Minot, a joint-use airport with both a commercial and a military side, it was late enough in the day that the control tower had closed for the night already. We had to cancel our IFR[50] clearance and finish the flight under Visual Flight Rules (VFR).[51] That's not a big deal, but we rarely fly VFR in the military. We got down safely and had to taxi ourselves as well. The crew gave me a slight scare when they pulled up so close to a smattering of small civilian aircraft that one of our sprawling wings completely overlapped a parked Cessna.

None of us made it to bed before 1:00 a.m.

---

50. Instrument Flight Rules, under ATC's radar control.
51. Visual Flight Rules, where pilots control themselves and require little or no assistance from ATC.

Transponders

Tech Tab #5

Radar has been around since before World War II, but has become much more elaborate over the last eighty-five years. The word "radar" is an acronym for **RA**dio **D**etection **A**nd **R**anging, coined by the US Signals Corp in 1939. A *primary* radar signal is one that is sent out, bounces off a target, and returns the same signal back to the originating device. The time it takes the signal to return is calculated by an algorithm, which is then displayed as a blip on the controller's oscilloscope screen.

In the jet age, rather than rely wholly on radio waves bouncing off metallic surfaces, a secondary, more precise (and reliable) radar is needed to pinpoint a 3-dimensional view of the hundreds of aircraft in the sky concurrently. Consider the job of a controller managing as many as fifteen targets at a time. Spurious items can interfere with antiquated primary radar. A semi-truck traveling along a highway makes a big metallic target that can reflect a signal similar to a low-flying aircraft. Rain clouds and mountains can also create primary radar returns. These "false" cues could create havoc in trying to prevent midair collisions.

The solution: install a small radio in the aircraft that constantly sends out signals that add altitude (Mode C) to the location, distance and ground track already provided. This simple little device **TRANS**mits and re**SPOND**s to continuous queries from Air Traffic Control (ATC). When radar contact is established, a controllers screen picks up the target and links a data block that displays further info about the aircraft based on the pilot's filed flight plan. This creates a much more accurate picture on the radar screen, eliminating false returns and increasing safety. After all, the controller's sole job is to prevent airborne metal from striking other objects. A pilot enters an assigned, unique 4-digit code, or "*squawk*" into his transponder that distinguishes it from other aircraft in the area. If the transponder is inoperative, as in the case of our IL-76 in this story, a controller would have to rely on primary radar signals from a century ago, effectively eliminating several layers of safety. In our litigious society, no controller is likely to approve continued flight under such conditions. It would be like asking you to do without your smartphone today and relying on an old-fashioned, rotary-dial landline bolted to your kitchen wall.

Chapter 17 - Wrong Airport

Поживём — увидим
"We will live — we will see"

If you and I were together in my office right now, I could easily induce an authentic illusion in your brain in less than 90 seconds. I've done it dozens of times in classrooms. Though sight is by far the strongest of the three sensory inputs to mammalian spatial awareness, the other two signal-makers that let you and I know where we are and what position we are in at any given moment can interfere with our vision in such a way as to disorient us. (You can try this experiment at home with the help of a companion by following the instructions in the Tech Tab on the next page.)

That's why instructors pound into pilots' brains to "trust your instruments," referring to the onboard avionics that use scientific methods to provide in-flight position awareness. Disregarding these external inputs can quickly create spatial disorientation. Spatial D, as we call it, has led to many fatal accidents. My worst in-flight encounter with this powerful phenomenon caused havoc with my brain and literally incapacitated me.

In 1987, another instructor pilot and I were on a proficiency flight in the T-38 Talon. We stopped by a military operations area to practice aerobatics, and while performing a loop, Major Smith's map case popped open in the rear cockpit. A small 5″ x 8″ chart book fell out and lodged behind his ejection seat. As hard as he tried, Major Smith could not reach back far enough to grab the book to secure it. This wouldn't do, because it was a hot day and once we landed, we'd need to immediately pop open the canopy. Opening up before engine shutdown, though,

"Spatial D" at Home

Use any chair that spins freely all the way around. Keep it safe!

1. Have a person sit in the chair with their legs folded underneath them (they can't touch the floor), and their eyes tightly closed.

2. Instruct them to look up quickly and focus their eyes on a clock or picture on the wall when instructed. The room should be quiet.

3. With the subject's head cocked, ear laying on one shoulder, rotate the chair at a constant and fairly rapid speed and keep it going in one direction for about ten full rotations.

4. After ten rotations, stop the chair abruptly where the subject will be facing the before-mentioned focus object on the wall and have them stare intently at the clock or picture.

5. Let observers watch the subject's eyes closely. Their pupils will typically bounce rapidly from back and forth uncontrollably. This specific type of Spatial D is called nystagmus.

Key points:

- **Rotation protocol:**
  - Ensure rotations are in one direction at a constant, fairly rapid speed (no acceleration or deceleration)
  - After a set duration (ten spins), abruptly stop the chair.
- **Monitoring:** Closely observe the subject for any signs of discomfort, dizziness, or nausea and stop the experiment if any of these signs are present.
- **Feedback:** Ask the subject to describe their experience after the test. Most people get a real kick out of trying this!
- **Trade places:** Let the test operator take the subject's place and repeat the test.

NOTE: Official pilot training uses a special device called a Barany Chair to induce spatial disorientation. There are several types of disorientation, including the Coriolis illusion and the Graveyard spiral. All are caused by a mismatch between visual, vestibular (inner ear) and somatosensory (seat-of-the-pants) inputs to the brain. **Pilots must trust their cockpit attitude instruments** and ignore the overwhelming false sensations induced by Spatial D.

Watch a demo of a Barany chair at https://tinyurl.com/SpatialD

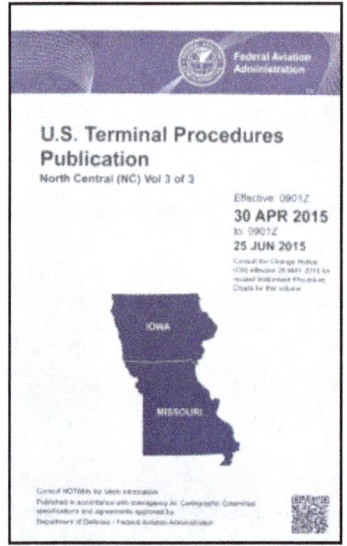

A book of charts like the one that fell out of our map case

could allow the charts to come loose in the wind and be sucked into the vacuum of the running engine, causing FOD damage. So I came up with a plan.

"John, I have the aircraft." I shook the stick slightly from the forward cockpit, physically signaling my control.

He raised both hands high so I could see them in my rear-view mirror and politely replied, "Rawjer, you have the aircraft." Positive transfer of aircraft control is vital; with dual controls, you can't afford any confusion as to who is flying the airplane.

"I'm going to push over to zero G's to dislodge the book," I said, "then hit the speed brake to propel it forward so you can grab it."

Understanding the plan, he held up his right hand, curved palm facing the back of the plane, ready to catch the chart. I pulled into an aggressive climb of about 20° nose up, then pushed over into a parabola to induce momentary weightlessness, hoping the errant book would float to the top on the rear canopy. Then I flipped the speed brake switch open on the throttle quadrant with my left thumb.

Slam! The deceleration was abrupt. It worked perfectly! The displaced publication slid along the top of the canopy and landed securely into Major Smith's open hand. "Got it!" he exclaimed.

However, at exactly that moment, we entered a layer of thick clouds I hadn't realized we were approaching so quickly.

All my senses were whacked at once. My fat head started bobbing up and down uncontrollably, alternating between my chin clanging onto my chest and my helmet thrusting hard to the rear, hitting the back of the head guard on my ejection seat. I was entirely incapacitated by spatial disorientation. I had no power to stop the chaotic spasming.

Inadvertently, our maneuvering had outsmarted my brain, and disparate inputs from all three positional sensory systems clashed into one big ball of confusion.

"You have the aircraft," I frantically yelled, recognizing that I was wholly incapable of piloting at that moment. My head banging must have only lasted a few seconds, but they were crucial seconds, and even after the bobbing stopped, my head needed time to clear.

When there's a mismatch in the signals from your vestibular system (inner ear), vision, and somatosensory system (seat-of-the-pants body awareness), strange things happen. I had tricked all three systems at once by: (a) inducing weightlessness, an abnormal sensation for the earth-bound human; (b) decelerating rapidly, causing unexpected changes in the circulation of fluids in the inner ear that disrupted my balance, and (c) simultaneously entering a cloud bank, denying any visual reference to the horizon. My brain rebelled, saying, "That does not compute," and threw a fit in the form of head banging!

This was a severe case of Spatial D, and it only ever happened to this degree once in my career. It was the perfect storm.

But there are many more subtle forms of disorientation. The "leans" is very common among aviators, as a slanting cloud layer can make you believe you are in a turn when you are not. By trusting cockpit instruments, pilots can maintain level flight, but their bodies will almost always imperceptibly lean in the opposite direction of the perceived turn.

One setup for disaster is the obvious "no-no" of landing on the wrong runway. Valuable ground references are available during fair weather approaches to an airfield, but when visibility is poor because of clouds or other atmospheric phenomena, radio or satellite navigational aids assist the pilot with indicators to ensure alignment with the correct runway. But, just as I could create internal turmoil in your brain through a simple exercise, nature can also conspire to play with an aviator's mind.

Aeroflot 387's pilot was not very experienced inside our National Airspace System. The Eastern Seaboard is one of the busiest air corridors in the world. Flight into or out of one of these bustling aerodromes requires intense concentration, concise communication with all players both in the cockpit and on the ground, accurate setup of navigational aids, and spot-on situational awareness. In addition, disciplined coordination between crew members is essential.

28 August 1991, Wednesday (continued)

As an early-to-bed kinda guy, I didn't hear all the scheming around the bar after our late arrival in Minot Tuesday night. Between the show organizers and the pilots, a risky deal materialized that failed to pass the sanity check. Our Soviet guests were out to please, and the airshow sponsors were intent on making up for lost time and wowing the public crowds.

At 5:15 a.m., the shrill ring of the hotel's bedside phone startled me.

"This is the wake-up you requested," came the smooth, lilting voice of the front desk receptionist. I had not asked for a call.

With little over four hours of sleep, the regulatory crew rest period had barely been half met.

Part one of the previous night's bar deal was already underway, and it was too late to rebuff their ill-laid plans. I couldn't mask my hot displeasure at the rude early start, but everyone on the team was now wide awake and there was no option to tell everyone to go back to bed. Who could sleep now anyway? Since I was fully roused, I was more than ready to get this last leg of our flight done. *"I'll be glad to finally get these guys to their destination,"* I thought. *"This has been one of those 'I can't take it any longer' type trips!"*

The schedule changes, money problems, maintenance issues, and long days had all balled up into one enormous heap of smoldering frustration. And now we were piling safety problems on top of it all. It could all blow up and cascade into severe, even perilous, challenges ahead.

Sitting at a hotel breakfast table alone, I ate my eggs, bacon, and toast absently, fingers tapping as I reflected on a time or two early in my flying career when I'd allowed a tight schedule to lead me to take shortcuts. By deviating from a normally precise preflight routine, serious mistakes followed — mistakes that could have killed someone. I decided not to let this current crew rest infraction go unchallenged. Despite the futility of an after-the-fact warning, I pulled the show organizers aside.

"Jim and Flip, you guys are pushing the crews too hard. I understand your desperation after all these delays, but this 'hurry up' attitude can cause mishaps. We have specific, rigid rules we have to follow. By law, and for everyone's safety, crew members are required to get eight hours of sleep. We'll get there. Don't force things."

Uninterrupted rest was how the regulation read, but I didn't bother to throw in that detail. The intent was for individuals to recuperate within that resting period. They still had the freedom to do their own thing. There's the added requirement of eight hours "from bottle to throttle,"[52] which hadn't been met in this case either. Flying is a hard business, and preservation of life means everyone needs to always be on top of their game. Alcohol and flying don't mix. Period.

Legally, I could have played hardball and demanded we wait another four hours before takeoff, but the damage was already done.

It was then that an even bigger bombshell dropped.

"Yeah, sorry about that," Flip acknowledged glibly as he pulled out his planner and spread it on the table. Continuing on, his tone was unapologetic. "We'll pay closer attention to crew rest in the future. We're sure excited about the arrival show in Cleveland today, though."

BOOM! Fireworks went off in my head. Part two of last night's after hours deal suddenly came to light.

"Arrival show? What do you mean?"

"The pilots of all three aircraft have agreed to do a low pass over the field at Cleveland with the IL-76, MiG-29s, and F-16 escorts in one big formation. Everyone's excited! We've informed the local press to expect it."

Another bar conversation I'd missed. Maybe I should take up drinking?

Sure, a thrilling aerial display would be cool. But such a spectacle would require FAA approval. Having put together such requests in the past, I knew there was no way it could happen on such short notice. I advised the organizers they had no authority to make such an arrangement, nor did the pilots. Then, just to be fair, I dutifully passed along their last-minute

---

52. In the USAF, this civilian rule is expanded to twelve hours.

request to FAA International. I kept the crew rest violation to myself.

"Colonel O'Toole, good morning. This is Captain Whicker. I'm with this Shotgun gaggle departing from Minot for Cleveland. Ummm ... don't get upset ... I know the answer, but I'm trying to appease these guys. They want to perform an unplanned and unrehearsed formation arrival show when we get to Cleveland later today."

Over the phone, I could feel unmistakable tension as his blood pressure surely skyrocketed. Colonel O'Toole was a good friend of mine, and it wasn't hard to imagine him rising out of his chair in his DC office. The line picked up the definite sound of his fist slamming down on the desk.

"TELL THEM," *slam!* "THEY'RE OUT," *slam!* "OF THEIR FLIPPIN'," *slam!* "MINDS!" *slam!*

"Thank you, sir. That's all I needed to hear." His authoritative backing settled over me as a warm wave of relief. I passed along the unequivocal final word to the organizers and pilots. Jim's gaze dropped to the floor, and the air of excitement drained from everyone's faces. These crews were flying into an unfamiliar airfield, no one had had proper rest, and everyone was overly stressed from the change of plans out of Anchorage, the lack of fuel at Comox, the inoperative transponder, and having to turn back. Then there had been the unplanned overnight stay at Minot.

The show coordinators wanted to make their exhibit a success, but we could not allow any further compromises. Accidents don't generally happen because of a single mistake. Rather, they often result from a sequence of individual events compounded, one after another. This was where we broke that chain!

Impulsivity is one of five recognized hazardous attitudes

pilots tend to manifest.⁵³ These well-known character flaws are inherent in the profession and must be guarded against. Any of them can lead to in-flight tragedy. Instead of taking a moment to think things through to the best alternative, a pilot with an impulsive attitude takes the first option that comes to mind — whatever sounds exciting or expedient.

By that well-placed phone call to the FAA, we effectively put on the brakes, thought things through, and quashed any prospect of a shoddy, unrehearsed arrival show. There would be plenty of daring aerial prowess and fantastic showmanship displayed during the actual exhibition, where proper planning, preparation, and safety nets were in place.

Still, I was concerned. The more I contemplated what lay ahead today, the more my head spun. Was this IL-76 crew equipped to even handle an ordinary approach to the busy Cleveland area? Fatigue was already a factor, as was their inexperience in congested airspace. Things happen quickly flying into a big city: switching radio frequencies, turns to new headings, dynamic altitude clearances, aircraft configuration changes, speed adjustments, traffic advisories, multiple runways, and a general need to possess what we call SA — situational awareness.

And of course, added to the expected flailing involved with flying into a major American city comes the most difficult maneuver at the end of every flight: the landing. Just when you reach the limits of your physical and mental endurance comes the moment when your reflexes must be at their very best.

The build-up to this MiG Friendship Tour was pressuring everyone to push the envelope too far. Luckily, we had perfect

---

53. The others are machoism, resignation, being anti-authority, and having a deluded sense of invulnerability.

weather, thirty miles of visibility, daylight conditions, no turbulence, and a completely dry runway. If bad weather had played a role, I would have had the grit to postpone the flight. But the peer pressure, political, social, and economic demands to press on were overpowering.

Runways have large painted numbers that allow the pilot to remain oriented during an approach to ensure his actual bearing corresponds with the intended landing strip..

The Cleveland area, where we were landing, has a somewhat unique layout. It sports two large airports within ten miles of one another, each with two parallel runways. Runways on both airfields are pointed in the same direction and thus have identical numeric names: Runway 24 (see Tech Tab 6: *Runway Names*, on next page).

Cleveland-Hopkins International (CLE), the larger of the two, lies inland five short miles south of Lake Erie. Burke Lakefront (BKL), our intended destination, sits on the shoreline, slightly north and east of the international airport.

Pilots landing to the west at CLE are cleared to land on either the left (24L) or right (24R) runway. Navigational aids help crews line up on the extended centerline of the cleared runway. This allows two aircraft to approach and land simultaneously. Perhaps you've been a passenger on an airline and enjoyed the beauty of watching another plane flying right alongside you just before landing.

Nearby, Burke's parallel runways have exactly the same designators: 24L and 24R. A separate tower controls their traffic on an entirely distinct radio frequency. Even so, it's possible to confuse the two adjacent airports on approach unless you are situationally aware.

"SA" was not part of this IL-76 crew's repertoire. Basic flying skills were in short supply as we neared the big city of Cleveland,

Runway Names

Large airports utilize the efficiency of multiple parallel runways. Why? To allow two or more aircraft to land simultaneously, allowing more traffic in and out of the facility. Also, if a runway closes for any reason, another is still available. Additionally, this setup allows slow, general aviation aircraft to mix more easily with large airliners.

International airports require a minimum of 700 feet, or approximately 1/8th of a mile, lateral distance between runway centerlines. This allows for either aircraft on approach to have a little wiggle room for deviation left or right of the runway centerline. However, airports servicing only smaller Category I or II aircraft only need 300 feet lateral separation — not much room for error. Besides the proximity of two fast-moving machines, parallel runways present a potential for mistaken identity when an inexperienced pilot sets up to land, especially at an unfamiliar field. A pilot must maintain exceptional situational awareness to ensure he or she is lined up with the correct runway.

Runways are numbered by the magnetic course they are aligned to. If you land directly to the north, your course on touchdown is 360° on the compass. By removing that last digit, you come up with the name for this particular slab of concrete: Runway 36.

Tech Tab #7

Similarly, landing to the south puts you on Runway 18.

"But wait a minute," you say. "Since parallel runways are laid out along the exact same course and you are cleared to land on Runway 36, how do you know which of the two is yours?" The landing phase of flight is the most task-intensive of a pilot's duties, so let's Keep It Simple, Sherlock! The magic solution derived decades ago is to call the runway on the left, "Rwy 36L" and, you guessed it, the other one "Rwy 36R." Controllers must specify with complete and specific wording which runway you are cleared for: "[Call Sign], you are cleared to land Runway 36 Left." There, in front of and below you, you'll see (assuming good visibility) the big, bold number/letter combination painted right on the runway approach end in bright white: "36L." You can't go wrong. Some airports even have a third parallel runway and simply name it 36C for "Center."

and as we lined up for our approach, the radio suddenly came alive.

"Aeroflot 387, Cleveland Approach. State your intentions. You just passed through the localizer," or extended runway centerline, "to Burke and you are three hundred feet above your assigned altitude."

Fully task-saturated by now, Boris, the aircraft commander, completely missed the radio cue. I jumped in.

"Cleveland, this is the safety escort for Aeroflot 387. Request vectors for a new attempt at the approach." The embarrassment of sharing the same cockpit as these guys was extreme and surely must have carried over into the tone of my voice.

Not only could Boris not stabilize his altitude within two hundred feet of his assigned altitude, but he couldn't seem to keep his heading within several degrees of the requested heading. Missing an important turn like this in congested airspace was not acceptable. Was he hung over from last night or just exhausted from lack of sleep? His airmanship couldn't be this bad, could it? One might expect such loutish flying from a student pilot, but not from the captain of an international aircrew.

"Aeroflot 387, expedite to 9,000; turn right immediately to tree-one-zero[54] degrees for traffic avoidance."

We were being sent around the penalty box for our indiscretion.

Boris responded this time. "Aeroflot 387, climbing to 9,000 and turning to tree-one-zero." As we started the turn, I saw another "heavy"[55] jet on final approach to Hopkins uncomfortably close on our left. We had blasted through the required safety margin of separation from a Delta flight full of paying passengers.

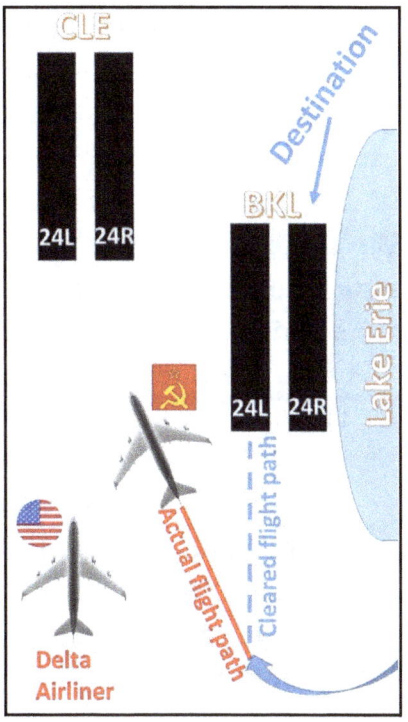

By now, I was standing tense and erect behind the two pilots, one hand on each of their seat backs to steady myself. I thrust my long arm between them, leaned forward, and forcefully gestured, almost touching the windscreen. "There! THERE's our airport! You were setting up for the wrong runway!"

Boris likely didn't understand the emphatic English I spurted, but there was no mistaking my meaning.

---

54. In the phonetic alphabet, three numbers are pronounced differently than in normal English: "tree" for 3; "fife" for 5; and "niner" for nine. Each digit of a directed compass heading is always spoken separately and distinctly to avoid confusion; rather than "three ten" degrees, a controller says "tree-one-zero."
55. For wake turbulence considerations, a "heavy" is defined as an aircraft with a maximum gross takeoff weight of 300,000 pounds or more. A "super heavy" has a GTOW of over a million pounds.

Cleveland Approach broke through again. "Delta 527 ... uh, we're going to have to send you around because of Aeroflot's violation inbound into Burke. Climb and maintain 7,000, turn left to one-fife-zero."

Pure dismay sounded in the Delta captain's reply. "Rawjer, Cleveland. Delta 527 climbing to 7,000, turning left to one-fife-zero. That's okay ... we had plenty of fuel to burn needlessly ... and no one on board has a connecting flight to worry about ..."

Ouch! The sarcasm felt like a knife in the gut.

Throughout this ordeal, I pondered some painful What Ifs:

- **What if** we had tried to get here with no working transponder? The erratic flying, coupled with an inoperative tracking mechanism, would have put us in a very compromising situation, possibly leading to loss of property or life.

- **What if** we'd been in IMC (instrument meteorological conditions), in the clouds, without reference to the ground? Although most instrumentation is common to aircraft across the world, there are enough subtle differences in Soviet avionics[56] that would make it impossible for me — seated sideways behind the pilots, and with a significant language barrier — to be of any help.

- **What if** we'd allowed their unrehearsed fancy arrival show at Burke? They'd have surely scattered Cleveland-Hopkins traffic all over kingdom come because of their inexcusable

---

56. Soviet altimeters are in meters, whereas American aircraft measure altitude in feet. Their altimeter settings were calibrated to millibars of atmospheric pressure rather than inches of mercury, as are ours.

gaffe! Their sloppy execution of what should have been a very uncomplicated visual approach proved that Colonel O'Toole's prohibition of such a spectacle was indeed wise.

Finally, after a go-around, it was over. We landed ... and at the correct airport!

Despite the harried last twenty-five minutes of the flight, the long-awaited Soviet entourage received an amiable Midwest reception as they ambled out of the plane. The words of Mr. Ermakov hardly told the story as he told the press, "We're glad to finally be here."

No one noticed the sweat pouring down my forehead or heard our scrambled heartbeats pounding through our chests. How could anyone on the ground know we'd been floundering through the air like imbeciles, forcing ATC to scatter airliners just to keep them out of our way?

No, all they saw was a severely delayed group of international superstars coming to provide a spectacular airshow never before seen in America. Thankfully, those receiving our esteemed visiting crew only caught the glamour and missed the dirty, ugly part of making the sausage that finally got us there more than a week late.

Jon and I took a taxi to CLE to catch an immediate flight home. This one "short" trip had consumed eleven days of my life and become by far the longest, most complicated, and most nerve-wracking of my entire experience with the Shotgun program.

Except for the highlight of getting to know MiG pilot Alexander Garnaev, the entire episode was a flop in my book. However, that one new bond was well worth the hassle.

Chapter 18 - Wasted Runway

Из песни слов не выкинешь
"You cannot erase words from a song"

Five billion passengers a year board airplanes, fly thousands of miles, and land at their desired destination as if on a magic carpet. Often, this miraculous feat happens with no reference to the ground between takeoff and seconds before touchdown. Even with modern global positioning, imagine trying to do the same in your car, blindfolded. It can't be done. Why? Because navigation depends on visual references and GPS alone isn't adequate.

Flying over a cloud layer, terrestrial clues don't exist. Instead, crucial radio signals guide a trained pilot. Both ground- and space-based navigational aids make "blind" flight safe. Drift just one degree off course, and you'll end up one full mile from your destination after only sixty miles of travel! Airmen must have deep respect for instrument guidance. Strict attention to this proven technology is critical.

11 September 1991, Wednesday

On today's trip into Gander, the plan was for the Soviets to drop us off, refuel, and then continue to their homeland. My Shotgun partner and I were to spend the night at Marg's Cape Cod B&B and head home the next morning.

The weather in Newfoundland is wet and cool. There are only sixty-one days of sunshine in Newfoundland , with forty-six inches of precipitation per year. Having a warm and inviting place to go after an exhausting flight was important to us, not to mention having good, friendly folk to talk to.

Weather Minima

Tech Tab #8

A pilot often doesn't have the luxury of landmarks to guide him on his journey because 2/3 of the earth is typically covered by clouds at any given time. To get the job done and keep customers happy, he may lose sight of the ground as early as 200' above the ground after takeoff. The entire trip could be made without visual references. Hopefully, she'll pick up the destination runway in the final descent by somewhere around 200' AGL.

This feat can only done by use of either ground- or space- based navigational aids that send out precise radio signals that translate into readings on his instrument panel.

Pilot training pounds into your very being that you must TRUST your instruments! Because, as previously shown in the Spatial D Tech Tab (pages 142-143), your body's method of orienting itself in space has fatal flaws built in.

In trusting those instruments, pilots are also taught not to exceed safety margins built into such readings. For instance, if you are approaching through the weather, published guidance only allows you to descend to a certain altitude before you MUST either visually see the airport OR go around the traffic circuit to try again! That is, you must stop the descent, apply power, raise the nose, and begin a climb away from the invisible ground. Doing anything else is just plain dangerous, as your descending aircraft could easily hit an obstacle or the ground. Disregarding altitude restrictions is foolhardy.

Minimum Descent Altitudes (MDAs) are hard limits specific to non-precision approaches. A non-precision approach only provides horizontal guidance – no vertical guidance. MDA is an absolute floor; descending even one foot below it is a bust. It constitutes an extremity through which no one is authorized to continue without positive visual acquisition of the runway environment.

During a precision approach, both horizontal (alignment with the landing runway) and vertical (glide slope) guidance are present. The minimum altitude allowed on this type of approach is generally lower and is represented by Decision Height (DH). It is a decision point, through which you will necessarily bust several feet as you make the transition from a descent to a climb. MDAs and DHs are published, certified restrictions that are a law unto aircrews.

The forecast on the day of our arrival showed a low overcast with absolutely no breaks in the clouds down to four hundred feet above the ground, not at all unusual. The prevailing winds demanded we approach from the south to land to the north on the 10,200-foot Runway 3. A precision approach was impossible because of the lack of glide slope equipment on board the aircraft, so we made a non-precision localizer-only approach, with only horizontal positioning left and right of the extended centerline — no vertical guidance. We had to make stairstep descents and level-offs rather than riding a smooth, continuous, elevator-like letdown.

Staying in perfect alignment while in the clouds is crucial to setting up for a safe landing. Per the certified procedure, and without the added precision guidance of a glide slope indicator, we could legally only descend to 760 feet MSL, equivalent to 332 feet above the ground. If we could see the runway environment (lights, buildings, or roads), by the time we reached that altitude, continued descent was authorized. Descending any lower than 332 feet AGL without breaking out of the clouds would not only be illegal, it would be downright foolhardy and dangerous! These procedures are set up and carefully tested to ensure that an aircraft that follows published altitude restrictions will never run into a man-made or natural obstacle while flying blindly in weather. (Research has proven that plowing into granite or other immovable objects is generally not advisable.)

Outside the town of Gander is a prominent reminder of just how dangerous it is to disregard aircraft and weather limitations. This airport was the location of Canada's worst air disaster in history: an Arrow Air crashed on takeoff in 1985, killing 248 US servicemen and eight crew members on their way home from Egypt after serving six months on a peacekeeping mission on the Sinai Peninsula.

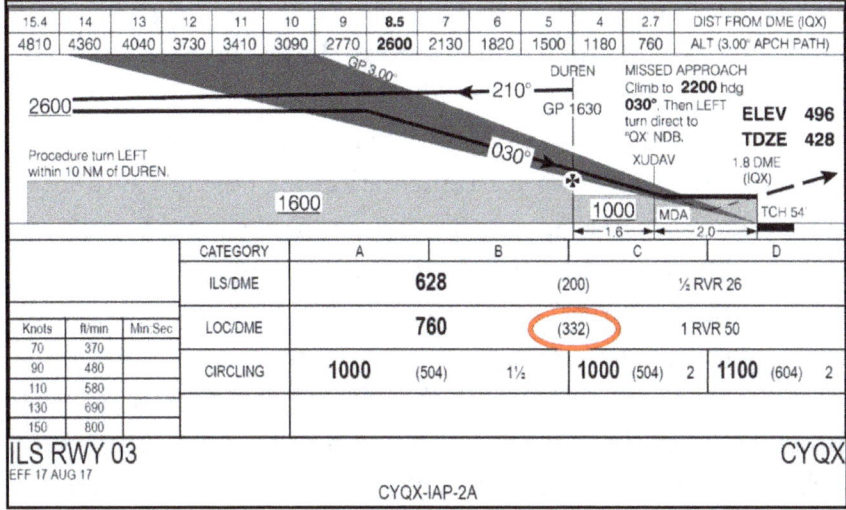

Gander WX Minima Chart for our Non-Precision Approach

As trained aeronauts, the Soviets well know the international standards of instrument flight rules. They are fully cognizant of the rationale behind altitude minimums published by aviation authorities. However, on this flight into Gander, I learned that this crew's mindset lacked the deep regard for safety that was drilled into my head in the United States Air Force.

As the crew set up for this run-of-the-mill approach and landing, I occupied my normal station next to the navigator. I had no legal duties nor jurisdiction now that we were outside US airspace, but my seat in the cockpit was more comfortable than sitting sideways in the parachute strap seats downstairs.

If I had been seated back in the passenger and cargo section, I would have never known anything was out of order.

There was no turbulence, and the light rain just slid off the windscreen immediately upon impact, giving the entire aircraft a nice fresh, free wash. There was no lightning to distract and no ice was building up on any part of the fuselage, wings, or engine nacelles to cause concern. A slight right crosswind was evident and easily manageable. Daylight prevailed, so the only visual restriction was the thick nimbostratus clouds reported to extend from four hundred feet above the ground to almost 17,000 feet MSL. "In the soup" for a full fourteen minutes on our approach, we would rely solely on instrumentation for position awareness. If the forecast was accurate, this was no big deal; we'd break out almost a hundred feet before our minimum descent altitude. Every pilot in the world would kill for such textbook instrument-flying practice.

I was eager to be done with the trip so I could get back to my family. This job kept me away far too much, and with five little girls growing up into beautiful young women right before my eyes, every moment I could spend with them and my wife was precious.

I had almost checked out mentally, but I casually glanced at the cockpit instruments and noticed something subtle, but unusual. These guys weren't handling the slight crosswind very well. They consistently allowed the aircraft to be blown slightly to the left of the runway centerline, and they weren't making any corrections. They seemed perfectly satisfied with their lackadaisical flying. No proud pilot in his right mind would allow such deviation without making every effort to stay locked onto the approach path.

I decided to pay closer attention. It was my life on the line here and if they messed this up and ended up hitting something while navigating through this pea soup weather, I'd never see my beautiful wife or daughters again.

My body unconsciously tensed as I leaned to the right, willing the aircraft back onto centerline. It took all my willpower to keep from putting on my instructor hat and yelling at this flawed student-like pilot who somehow missed the lesson on precision.

Deep into the descent, I reviewed the approach plate used by the crew. Cross-checking the altimeter, I saw we were passing through 2,300 feet, still a good 1,500 feet above the ground, well within the safety zone.

But why weren't they being more assertive about creeping to the right, as the instruments are practically shouting at them to do? If this had been an instrument training flight, I'd have flunked this crew on the spot for lack of aggressiveness. It was as if they weren't even trying!

We were only a minute and a half from touchdown. Under the circumstances, it would be uncomfortable to jink hard right after the runway came into view. We would be slowed for landing and low to the ground — a dangerous combination that could lead to a deadly stall.

1,800 feet and still slightly offset to the left, we had to either see the runway lights in the next 1,040 feet or go missed approach, a climbing turn to safe airspace away from the terminal and other obstacles.

Nothing was visible. The clouds blinded us.

1,000 feet. We were now at circling height, the lowest we could go if surface conditions required us to circle to land. Pilots sometimes use this method when there's no published instrument approach available to the desired runway. You flew to the opposite runway, then circled wide, making up to a full 180-degree turn to land against the prevailing wind.

Nothing visible!

Legally, we could descend another 240 feet, but the automated weather reporting system (AWOS) was saying the cloud ceiling had just dropped farther, completely negating the 400-foot overcast previously reported. That was a big complication that meant we'd have to go missed approach if we couldn't distinguish any features around the runway in the next several seconds.

Our alignment was still off. With considerable effort, I held my tongue, even though my brain felt like it was about to burst. I lifted myself halfway up in my seat, futilely attempting to penetrate the thick clouds with my non-existent X-ray vision. Runway lights, taxiway lights, approach lights — *any* visual cue would allow us to continue the descent. In this kind of weather, the tall rotating beacon should be blinking high above the airport buildings to help us acquire the airfield.

Descending at a rate of four hundred feet per minute, our absolute floor (the Minimum Descent Altitude, or MDA) would materialize in thirty-nine seconds. An MDA is a hard restriction. Technically, busting below it by even one foot constitutes a safety foul.

Unbelievably, there appeared to be no intent by the pilot to honor the published altitude restrictions. We were blowing right through the 760-foot limit. Was the crew so used to this type of flagrant rule-bending by their captain that they lived with such safety breaches regularly? Obviously, the culture surrounding this commander's personality discouraged crew member input. He seemed to be a law unto himself.

At **760 feet,** I could hold my frustration no longer and yelled out, "MINIMUM DESCENT ALTITUDE!" It was a required call that his crew mates dared not utter.

The pilot in command completely ignored my outburst. He was demonstrating two characteristics known to be flaws in pilots' personalities: anti-authority and invulnerability. It made for a dangerous cocktail of hazardous attitudes. His body was as tense as mine, concentrating on getting this aircraft on the ground, but perhaps he had a hot date tonight (or something) and knew he'd miss it if we took the time to go around and try another approach, especially since the ceiling seemed to drop by the minute.

An additional looooong fifteen seconds passed, and now we were below the lower, precision Decision Height (DH), which was a mere **200 feet** above the ground. Descending this low would have been okay if the aircraft had been equipped appropriately, but it was not.

There was still nothing visible and our own anti-collision strobe lights reflected off the shroud of clouds that engulfed us, causing a sort of hypnotic effect.

I yelled out again, completely out of my jurisdiction, "DECISION HEIGHT! *Let's go missed approach!*" but this guy was determined — and foolish. There was no lack of fuel, no reason to put anyone's life in danger. He was counting on breaking out of the clouds at any second so he could set this monstrous machine on the ground and be done with it. I was afraid we'd all be done, once and for all!

We were now fifty-eight feet lower than any of the approaches allowed under any circumstance, and with nothing but thick clouds visible, this guy was still descending. I yelled again, "GO AROUND!!" this time with a tone of command, though I may have inadvertently let a slight burble of anxiety show in my voice.

It was somewhat like driving down your home street without having scraped your windshield after a winter storm, hoping you don't hit anything. As an evaluator, I knew that a US pilot who pulled such a stunt would be grounded immediately, disciplined, and required to get remedial retraining. We don't put up with blatant disregard for rules, especially when safety is compromised.

At just **165 feet** above the ground, and with the instrument needle depicting the runway centerline still deflected to the right, and so close to the earth's hard surface, I decided the game was over. I was furious. Whether only in my head or out loud, I cannot say, but in my memory, my voice boomed over the intercom as I demanded, **"Take this thing around if you ever hope to fly in the US again."** The pilot probably didn't understand my English, and I wasn't fluent enough in Russian to even come up with that statement in his language, but he knew my meaning by the intensity of my temper and my hot breath down his neck.

At that very moment, just **100 feet** above the ground, too close to *terra firma* to safely make any horizontal adjustments to our skewed flight path, and with my whole body sweating in pure anticipation of crashing, we suddenly broke out of the clouds and saw the airport lights. The beautifully laid out asphalt was about 250 feet to the right of our flight path. He had to swerve abruptly while still descending, at a dangerously slow airspeed, with less than ten seconds to touchdown.

It was not pretty. It was not safe. And it did not end well.

As I braced for landing, it looked like we were still seventy-five feet to the left of the centerline, even after that dangerous last-second sidestep. *Kerplunk!* We were on the ground. The commander smoothly pressed the right rudder to coax the aircraft back toward the safety and comfort of that gratifying white dashed centerline.

We'd made it. We were alive. But I still harbored ill thoughts, especially toward the PIC (pilot-in-command). He'd put twelve souls, as we call them in the aviation community, in danger for no good reason. We could easily have gone around and tried again, or we could have flown to St. John's, a wide-open divert base that was a mere one hundred nautical miles away. There was no excuse for his blatant lack of airmanship.

As we taxied to the terminal, I unstrapped and gathered my belongings. No longer wishing to associate with those guys, I wanted to separate myself before I said anything I might regret. I'd submit an official complaint to both Aeroflot and the FAA.

This crew deserved a reprimand.

After engine shutdown, I was the first to whip down the cockpit ladder, all of my worldly goods slung over my shoulder. It surprised me to see the airport manager's vehicle, along with several others, approach our plane with their emergency lights flashing. It seemed quite the overkill to welcome a Soviet flight that was by now so commonplace in Gander. What was even more perplexing was that they all appeared to be peering at the left landing gear. I twisted my head around to follow the direction of their gaze.

The object of concern became immediately apparent and stopped me in my tracks. Another surge of adrenaline raced through my body as I realized just how lucky we all were to be in one piece!

By now, the PIC had also lowered himself to the ground. The airport manager quickly stepped into his path and bluntly asked,

"Did you guys land off the runway?"

Standing to the side and behind the pilot, in full view of the airport authority, my head bobbled up and down in an exaggerated affirmative nod.

"Of course not!" replied the rotund commander. "Why do you ask?"

The authoritative Canadian manager didn't flinch. He merely pointed to the left main landing gear with a weighty gesture. There, one could plainly see mud and grass stuck between the tires and rims of several outboard wheels. "Your gear obviously shows that your left mains touched down in the grass. And to boot, there are glass shards all over the runway at the 1,500-foot mark where your tires ran over and destroyed at least five runway edge lights as you steered back onto the tarmac! We'll have to close the runway for at least twenty minutes while the sweepers go out and clean up your mess. You'll need to come with me to file a report. Would you like our mechanics to inspect your landing gear for any damage?"

Extremely embarrassed, unable to escape the proof or to "unwrite the song" he had just sung, the pilot stooped slightly as he replied, "No, thanks. We have our own specialists on board who can check the airplane over."

IL-76 with left mains off the runway

With that, I was off. I shook my head incredulously as I walked toward the military side of the terminal. Thanks to the split international configuration of the facilities, I wouldn't have to speak or associate with this crew again. They went their way, and I called a cab to slip away to my comfortable oasis, the Cape Cod B&B. I could review the day's excitement from the solace of a well-kept home environment while eating a lovely, hot meal prepared by our gracious host, Marg.

This whole experience produced just one positive result: It was right then that I determined I would someday write a book about all the unusual flight experiences I was having while performing Constant Shotgun duties with the Soviets. *No one may believe me*, I thought, *but some of these stories are simply too good to be forgotten. History needs to know.*

POSTSCRIPT: Years after this incident, Lt. Colonel Al Westrom, my boss at the USAF Special Activities Center, shared with me a similar encounter he'd experienced. I had no idea until then that mine was not an isolated event.

I arrived at Gander Airport in Newfoundland to pick up a Soviet Special Flight the next day. As always, I went down into the airport operations office to use their AUTOVON line to call the Pentagon Ops Center to tell them that I was in position for the flight. While I was down there, one of the Royal Canadian Mounted Police officers told me that he wanted to show me something.

We had always made a point of making friends with the staff at Gander, and they were unfailingly helpful and cooperative. The Mountie remembered me from previous flights and had me get into his official SUV. He got on the radio and talked to the tower and told them that he wanted runway access. We entered the runway about a third of the way from the approach end and he drove down the right side of the runway, which was the side away from the terminal area. The runway was clear, but there was still a lot of wet snow on the ground.

I really had no idea what we were doing, and he said, "I want you to see what your Russian friends did." We drove to about halfway down the runway and he said, "There." He was pointing to the right side. There, it was obvious, because of the very clear tire tracks, that a large aircraft had gone off the runway, into the snow and mud. All the gear had been off the runway. Then he pointed out where the aircraft had come back onto the runway. The gear had left troughs of discarded snow and mud, little ridges of it. We followed it onto a taxiway, and then the detritus led all the way up to an IL-86 that was parked on the ramp and loading passengers for departure.

We drove up, and I rolled down the window of the SUV. We could hear the snow and slush still falling off the high gear, wings, and fuselage.

"Colonel, are you going to fly on that plane?"

"No, my flight's tomorrow."

"Is there something we should do about this?"

"Sell our Aeroflot stock?"

Chapter 19 - Engine Lost!

В тихом омуте черти водятся
"Still waters are inhabited by devils"

5 November 1991, Tuesday

While meeting and briefing two new Shotgunners, Lieutenants White and Brown (their real surnames) in the morning, I got word that the next day's trip was being pushed to Friday, which really messed up my plans. Then, in the evening, I received notification of a possible mission to the USSR that weekend as well! It was getting progressively harder to cover the increasing number of Soviet flights. All of the easing of tensions were creating a *lot* of business. What originally had been set up to cover two trips a year to/from the UN for the Soviet delegations was now overwhelming us with "official" and government flights.

6 November 1991, Wednesday

I received confirmation of the weekend's pop-up trip coming out of Moscow, and it was to be another AN-225 flight. As full-time Shotgunners, Greenie and I had to cover it.

The scramble began. We needed to get our visas immediately and depart from Dulles airport by 6:50 p.m. I didn't at all mind getting a second crack at flying that gargantuan airplane. James Auclair agreed to replace me on the AN-124 that had been bumped to Friday. Thank goodness he was so flexible!

Unfortunately, our principal contact at the State Department, Becky Joyce, was on leave, so we had to go through her substitute for the required diplomatic paperwork. That took extra time because her alternate wasn't as familiar with the process. Finally, with the needed letter in hand, we rushed to the Soviet Consulate on Phelps Place, NW DC. They told us they hadn't received any word of this AN-225 flight and we'd have to come back after 4 p.m. while they researched it.

"That isn't good enough," I complained. "We have to catch a flight at 6:50 to support your own country's request, and waiting until 4:00 to get our visas won't cut it."

"Okay, get here at 3:00." And with that one-hour reprieve, we were out the door.

The constant cloud of confusion we worked in really bothered me, and it was only getting worse. A mere seventeen-mile trek back to our office in DC can take forever, and a round trip to the consulate was pure torture.

We rushed to Greenie's house so he could pack. Thankfully, I had come already packed that morning, just in case. We quickly made hotel reservations and other arrangements, sent the obligatory secure message to our embassy in Moscow notifying them of our arrival, and tried to iron out a few other details for other upcoming Shotgun missions.

On our way back to get the visas, I asked my traveling companion about his experience at the Defense Language Institute, the very place I'd always wanted to go for some real language training. He'd just arrived at our detachment last summer after graduating from there in Russian.

"It's intense," is all he'd say. To this day, I'm not sure how, as a rated flight officer, he even got the chance to attend the school. It was rare, as most of their school appointments went to enlisted folks. The path to get there eluded me all those years.

Traffic slowed us so we didn't get to the consulate until 1615L after all, a mere two and a half hours prior to takeoff. With twenty-six miles yet to go in afternoon DC rush hour, it's no wonder I developed blood pressure issues in this job! Thankfully, the consulate had received confirmation of the trip just thirty minutes before our arrival, so had we made it back at 1500L, we'd have just been waiting around anyway. Our visas were ready.

7 November 1991, Thursday

We got little sleep on the overnight flight to Frankfurt, Germany. Our three-hour layover there turned into four, so by the time we arrived in Moscow, it was 1630L and already getting dark. Our reservation for the night was at the Radisson hotel, but our taxi driver couldn't find it! What we didn't realize was that all the changes in the Soviet Union made the modern Slavjanskaya Hotel, completed only one year before, the very first American-managed hotel in the country. Locals were not privy to that fact and only knew it as the славянская. Once we clarified that Radisson ran the place, the cabbie figured out exactly where to take us. It was extremely nice lodging but surrounded by serious intrigue[57] in those early days of Moscow's transition into the free market.

We were already dead tired but didn't want to waste any time since this was Greenie's first visit to Moscow and I hadn't been able to scope things out when I was there in March. Our timing was horrendous, though. Because of the incredible upheaval underway in the government, this was the first year since 1919 (with a few exceptions during war) that the gigantic annual Военный Парад, the October Revolution Day Parade, did not take place on this very date, 7 November! What a spectacle that

---

57. https://www.nytimes.com/1996/11/04/world/us-entrepreneur-is-gunned-down-in-moscow.html

would have been! Just one year before, the parade had featured massive amounts of military equipment and an assassination attempt on the life of President Gorbachev.

Most of the street vendors were closed for the holiday, as were Lenin's tomb, St. Basil's Cathedral, and the famous state-run department store, G.U.M.[58] in Red Square. Disappointed, we still marveled at the beauty and massiveness of those famous icons.

8 November 1991, Friday

Due to delays, we had another full day to look around Moscow. We first went to the US Embassy to talk to the air attaché and enlist his help finding the right people to coordinate our hotel pickup for the airport the next morning. Since it was still a holiday, it was tough to make contact with anyone. We finally found a nice secretary, Panja, at the Ministry of Aviation, who did her best to help us. As we went sightseeing throughout the city, we kept checking back with her, and each time, she'd come up short.

Our first stop after the embassy was the Soviet Army Museum. That building crammed a lot of Russian history into one spot. I thoroughly enjoyed all of it. The highlight, though, was when Greenie took a few photographs of me in front of the wreckage of Gary Powers' U-2 aircraft that was shot down on 1 May 1960 over Sverdlovsk. I'll bet I was the first U-2 pilot ever to see that wreckage since Gary himself! It was quite a thrill.

I learned the Soviets acknowledged that their first SA-2 missile downed their own MiG aircraft that had been trying to

---

58. https://gumrussia.com/ (Gosudarstvenny Universalny Magazin, State Department Store)

Gary Powers' U-2 Wreckage, Moscow Military Museum

shoot down the American spy plane. American history books say that was the case, but I didn't think the Russians would admit it. Yet there was a plaque to that effect on the wall of the museum.

It was already getting dark at 3:45 p.m., but we continued exploring by going to Red Square. Lenin's tomb was still closed, so we missed seeing it again. St. Basil's Cathedral was closing just as we got there, so we didn't get to go through it either, and they didn't even light it up that night. Then, just as we were getting ready to go through G.U.M., it closed for the holiday.

We walked around and found the famous Arbat Street, where vendors sell their wares. With some good bargaining, I bought about ten matryoshka dolls for an average of about $7 each. Plus, I found Pam a nice painted lacquer box and the girls a painted pencil each. When I was there in March, I didn't get to do any quality shopping like that. At our last call to Panja at 1830L, she informed us she had to go home but someone would call with a pickup time. There was nothing we could do but keep pressing forward.

Glenn shopping, downtown Moscow

We had an interesting dinner in one of the better restaurants in town. I had my first taste of caviar — too salty and fishy for me! We also ate smoked salmon, smoked herring, and some strange-tasting cold meats. For drink, all they had to offer was coffee, tea, champagne, Pepsi, and mineral water. I chose the latter, and to my horror, it tasted horrible. I couldn't force it down. I don't know how you can ruin water, but they somehow managed. I ended up having to drink Pepsi because I was drying up.

While we were sitting at our table, a young woman walked up to our table, flashed a pornographic magazine in our faces, and asked, in English, if we would like to buy a copy of the very first issue of the Russian Playboy.[59] Once they opened up to freedom of expression, an awful lot of pornography started showing up on the streets. It was surprising how quickly their system morphed in both good and bad ways.

---

59. Turns out Playboy did not introduce their magazine in Moscow until 1995, so this must surely have been a local copycat endeavor.

We returned to our hotel at 2130L a little worried because we still had no definite word about a pickup. Thankfully, the front desk had received a message just a half hour earlier that gave us the name and number of a man to call. He told us to be in the lobby at 5 a.m. That would make for a quick night!

9 November 1991, Saturday

We arose at 0400L to catch our military escort by 0500L, and our guy was right where he said he'd be. After paying our $225 per night hotel bill, we got in his jeep for the fifty-minute ride to Chkalovsky Air Base near Shcholkovo, thirty-one miles northeast of Moscow. It was the same place Frank Peluso and I had visited in March, but this time, the secrecy factor had diminished substantially — there were no curtains drawn across the car windows. They took us directly to a very nice waiting room and gave us a breakfast snack while we waited.

The crew eventually came and told us they'd be a little late getting off. Scheduled for 0700L, we finally broke ground at 1130L. Then, partly because of 140 knot headwinds, the eleven-hour flight took us twelve.

Greenie and I were just passengers prior to entering US airspace, but I still wore my headset in the crew rest compartment. I heard ATC in Reykjavik, Iceland, come over the radio.

"Aeroflot 387, Reykjavik Control Center."

"Reykjavik, this is Aeroflot 387. Go ahead."

"387, we have a request here to change your destination from Newark to JFK, over."

"Uh, hold on, Reykjavik. We need to consult with our US Air Force escorts."

Change our destination? Our routing had been pre-approved

at so many levels! Diverting was not possible, short of an emergency. One of the most important reasons we were onboard as escorts was to ensure no route deviation occurred.

The navigator, Sergei, who spoke almost perfect English, left his station in the cockpit to confer with me. He was as puzzled as I was and nodded in agreement as I told him that was impossible. JFK would only shorten our trip by 8 nm.

However, I did hedge, "I'll tell you what, Sergei. I'll call our contact at FAA International to confirm."

I scrambled up to the cockpit for access to the HF radio. High Frequencies are often full of static and can make communication extremely difficult, but they reach incredible distances. It was my only hope of getting through to Washington, DC. I called the Pentagon Ops Center and, because it was a Saturday, had them patch me directly to Lt. Col. O'Toole's home phone.

The connection was iffy. "Colonel, this is Shotgun Captain Whicker somewhere over the North Atlantic. How do you read?"

"Glenn, I can barely hear you. What's up?"

"Sir, Reykjavik Center is telling us to change our destination to JFK."

"No! They must proceed as previously cleared. NO CHANGES ARE AUTHORIZED! Is that understood?"

"Yes, sir, loud and clear. Shotgun out." The connection dropped. I'll bet he thoroughly enjoyed having his leisurely Saturday afternoon disturbed, especially when I already knew the answer. I was glad to have the bewilderment behind us.

"I guess you heard the man, Sergei. Our destination remains Newark."

I went back to my perch in the rear cabin and took my headset off to let my brain rest for a bit before things got busy up front. It was not a good decision.

At some point during the flight, the monstrous six-engine aircraft carrying us developed an oil pressure problem with the #5 engine. They had shut it down. You'd think that the internal sound would have changed enough that anyone on the plane would recognize something drastic was happening, but somehow, neither Greenie nor I heard or felt anything. We were oblivious to the situation.

By the time I came up to the cockpit to take my position as we entered our country's sovereign airspace, Sergei leaned across the aisle, covered his microphone, lifted the left side of my headset, and shouted directly into my ear, above the roar of the airplane:

"Is it possible to take a shortcut to Newark?" He didn't explain why he was asking. After having just had that extended conversation about deviations not being allowed, I was perplexed.

"No, because we don't have the authority to change the flight routing without talking to the FAA. Besides, we're already proceeding pretty direct anyway."

He shrugged and went back to his work, reporting my answer to the aircraft commander. Brian tapped me on the shoulder. "Did you know #5 engine is shut down?"

I had no idea! I leaned over to Sergei and asked, "Does the reason you want a more direct route have anything to do with the fact that we have an inoperative engine?"

"Da," was all he said. Now the light bulb came on! They had been the ones to ask Reykjavik for the rerouting to JFK to shorten their flight by just a bit, due to the engine failure.

"Okay, then we can do it. Why didn't you mention that in

the first place?"

Checking the charts, I confirmed that by going direct from our present position to Newark, we wouldn't overfly any sensitive areas. Coordinating with ATC, it was easy to get our clearance updated.

But that wasn't enough. Some other problem had them worried. Losing one-sixth of their total thrust by this one engine not pulling its weight, coupled with the higher than usual headwinds we'd encountered the entire trip, the crew admitted to getting a "little low" on fuel. The extra drag imposed by the windmilling engine added to the hefty fuel consumption.

"Whicker, is landing to the south available?" They wanted to shorten the flight as much as possible, landing opposite the direction of all other traffic into a major air traffic hub. Though it was highly unusual and a bit embarrassing to make such a request, I did so. I figured it was better to disrupt the entire pattern than to have the famous Antonov 224 Mriya crash in some farmer's field because of fuel starvation!

"New York Center, Aeroflot 387 is getting low on fuel. Any way you could set us up to land on Runway 22?" I could just hear the other aircraft in this very busy sector shaking their heads, thinking, "Here go the Soviets again, stirring the pot."

Silence. I'm sure Center was conferring with Newark's approach control. After an awkward pause, they came back.

"Aeroflot 387, unless you declare an emergency, we cannot disrupt the traffic flow for you to land to the south."

I relayed this news to the crew. Because we were still a ways out, they didn't think it necessary to declare an emergency, but did want to ask for priority in landing. With five operating engines, they didn't think it necessary to report the fact that we were one engine short! Any engine out should automatically require emergency status in my mind.

"Rawjer, Center, 387 is just asking for priority landing with minimum fuel." I really couldn't tell just how tight the fuel situation was, but these guys were experts on this one-of-a-kind machine, and they knew their stuff. I had no choice but to leave it to their discretion.

As we got closer and started our descent, the entire crew began to get extremely antsy. They asked again if I could try to arrange for us to land to the south, and I again told them we could if we declared an emergency. I knew by their tone that fuel was now getting real skosh, so I asked them point-blank, "Do you want to declare an emergency?"

The pilot finally said, "Da."

So the world's largest aircraft was given vectors straight to the airport, against prevailing traffic. We landed with 12,000 kg of fuel remaining, which works out to 26,000 pounds — a very small reserve for such a big plane. International Civil Aviation Organization regulations require an international flight on an IFR clearance to carry enough fuel to arrive at their destination, proceed to an alternate field if necessary, and hold at an intermediate altitude for forty-five minutes. Though a modern wide-body airliner may only consume about 7,000 pounds of fuel per hour, the AN-225 gobbles up gas at an hourly rate of up to 48,000 pounds!

I noticed upon landing that each of the five working power plants had only about 1,500 kg left, while the inoperative engine still had 4,500 kg. I'm assuming that fuel must not have been transferable to the other engines, though I don't know why.

If I'm right that the 4,500 kg was not usable, it means we landed with a maximum of twenty-five minutes of flight time before we became a very heavy rock dropping out of the sky. Way too close for comfort!

Greenie did a great job translating for the crew while they

got customs and immigration matters taken care of aboard the airplane, and then he and I got off and managed a ride for ourselves over to the terminal. We found seats immediately on a short flight to DC and didn't even take time to change out of our flight suits before boarding.

After we arrived in DC, I walked through my own front door just after 2200L. I had been awake for over twenty-four hours, with only short catnaps on a crew bunk. It was good to be home. I was exhausted.

However, Pam had a message for me to call James Auclair, who was on the mission I would have originally been on in San Diego. He had a crew member of the AN-124 who wanted to defect to the States, and James didn't know what to do. I soon discovered that since he hadn't been able to contact me, he had called Lt. Colonel Al Westrom, my boss, and was instructed to call the FBI, which takes care of such matters. Thankfully, James handled things appropriately before I had to get involved. They thought they had the guy, Sasha, talked out of defecting.

10 November 1991, Sunday

James Auclair called again, and sure enough, his Shotgun flight arrived in Miami ... *without* Sasha! The guy actually went ahead and did it. Another defector from the Soviet Union had hit the streets of America.

Just a little excitement to keep things interesting, with an engine failure and a Soviet defection all on the same day!

Chapter 20 - Sentenced to Siberia

Кто рано встаёт, тому Бог даёт
"God gives to those who wake up early"

6 December 1991, Friday

My mother's fifty-eighth birthday.

I'd only been home thirty-six hours from another mission, trying hard to fight off the start of a head cold, when I got a call at the office.

"Captain Whicker," the voice on the other end of the line said, "we need a Shotgun crew to get to Khabarovsk immediately to pick up a high-priority charity support flight from there direct to San Francisco."

"Where's Khabarovsk?" I'd never heard of half the towns in the vast regions of the Soviet Union.

"It's in the Siberian Far East," the voice answered. "Look it up. The ICAO[60] identifier code is UHHH. Your escort pilots need to be in place by Monday for a Tuesday pickup."

I hung up. It was clear this flight was getting top priority, and it soon became obvious why. We had about one hour to put together visa applications and get them to the State Department before they closed for the weekend. Be in place Monday in a desolate, unheard-of city 6,000 miles away where there were only two flights in and out per week. It was time to scramble! My head cold immediately faded into the background.

"Brian," I muttered across the desk to my partner, "It looks like it's you and me again, buddy. There's no way to get anyone

---

60. International Civil Aviation Organization

else for this quick response. Do you happen to know where Khabarovsk is?"

He didn't.

Together, we pulled out an atlas and turned to the page showing the Far Eastern Siberian region. "There it is," I pointed. "I wonder if Siberia is as frigid and bleak as they make it out to be." I had read large parts of Solzhenitsyn's *The Gulag Archipelago* a few years before, and my mental picture of the area centered on the concept of forced labor camps, deprivation, starvation and brutal cold — a place of miserable banishment from society. How much of that image was valid?

I was worried our chances of getting visas through the complexities of Washington's system over a short weekend were slim to none; however, I soon discovered that the skids were well greased. This flight had the power of none other than former Soviet Foreign Minister Eduard Shevardnadze behind it. Though he'd resigned his political position the year before, he still had considerable international clout. With his personal push, we were able to easily cut through the normal red tape and get our visas virtually on the spot. We were ready to go by the end of the business day, with time to spare. Wow! So this was how politics worked! Impressive.

I booked a commercial flight to Anchorage with a layover in Salt Lake City, near where I grew up, and Brian and I found a commercial Aeroflot flight to Khabarovsk that left Anchorage Sunday night at 2115L Alaskan time. The exigency behind the mission would barely allow us a few hours of sleep. It was a classic case of jumping through hoops, complete with a time warp. I sensed this was going to be another stressful and maybe not-so-fun trip. My premonition proved on the mark, but I could never have predicted the weight of what was about to transpire.

7 December 1991, Saturday

I reluctantly said goodbye to my little family in the morning and grabbed a taxi to Reagan International airport in DC. I had arranged for my parents to pick me up from the Salt Lake airport and drive me the short fifteen miles to my boyhood home in Kaysville, Utah, for a quick hello. It was nice to give my mother a hug the day after her birthday and to see my dad and a couple of brothers, as well as my grandparents, whom I hadn't seen for several months.

The Salt Lake Valley enjoyed a balmy 42°F with relatively calm winds — perfect flying weather. After another five-hour flight to Anchorage, it was already the next morning by the time I got settled into the hotel. I had been on the road for over eighteen hours.

8 December 1991, Sunday

I went to church with one of my dad's friends in Anchorage. Over the course of his forty years of flying around the world with various airline and cargo outfits, he'd spent plenty of time here and had developed some strong bonds. They had me over for dinner after the service and fed me the best pink salmon I've ever tasted. Then I picked Greenie up from the hotel and we checked our baggage at the airport before turning in our rental car.

That night, I'd cross the International Date Line for the very first time going west, instantly losing a full eighteen hours and effectively jumping into the future. Our airplane became a veritable time machine, transporting us from Sunday night to Monday night in an instant.

After just a six-hour flight, we mysteriously touched down a full twenty-four hours later than when we had taken off. Pretty cosmic.

The Aeroflot trip was smooth, and they served us a decent meal. I had my first taste of the Soviet equivalent of Kool-Aid; it tasted and smelled like perfume!

9 December 1991, Monday

By chance, we were seated next to a US businessman on the plane to Khabarovsk.

"What in the world takes you to such a dismal outpost as Khabarovsk?" I asked, awed that any American besides us would visit there.

"I'm checking up on a commercial endeavor for Evergreen Airlines," Bob answered. "It's just a quick overnight stop." Evergreen's LOGAIR[61] enterprise regularly flew a 4,400 nautical mile route from Hong Kong to Anchorage required a refueling stop, and Khabarovsk split it nicely into two near-equal segments.

"Wow," I exclaimed. "I guess the Soviets really are turning capitalistic!" I had studied the underlying tenets of Gorbachev's *perestroika*, and it looked like he was serious in adopting elements of liberal economics. My father had long flown for a competing LOGAIR company, Saturn Airways, so I was familiar with the setup of such an airline.

"We'll see how it all works out," Bob continued. "It isn't going to be easy operating there; they have yet to establish a proper set of business norms that we can depend on. We're hopeful, though, because having our company refuel there rather

---

61. Logistics Airlift; basically, LOGAIR is the transport of cargo under US government contract.

than in Japan could save us big bucks in operational costs."

Money: it makes the world go 'round. Evergreen's ambitious plans seemed interesting, but inconsequential to me at the time. Little did I know that this brand-new enterprise would soon take on great importance to Greenie and me.

The Siberian town of Khabarovsk was home to over half a million people in 1991. It lies only nineteen miles from the eastern border of China in an area claimed alternately by both Russia and China over the ages. Though Khabarovsk isn't technically within the politically defined Federal District of Siberia, which lies much farther to the west, it is located well inside the confines of the more extensive geographic and historical area of the Soviet Union known as the Soviet Far East.

The mere mention of the word "Siberia" invokes a harsh sense of foreboding, and even before we landed, gray clouds began to smother the little light that the winter day had offered. December was not the best month to visit what seemed to me to be the coldest part of the civilized world. Their average low temp of -10° F was in stark contrast to the almost 50 degrees I'd enjoyed the day before in Salt Lake.

The political timing of our mission couldn't have been worse either. There was no way we could know that the world was only a little over two weeks away from the complete dissolution of the USSR. Within the next sixteen days, Gorbachev would step down as Chairman of the Supreme Soviet and President of the Union of the fifteen Soviet Socialist Republics.

Of course, the regime had been in decline for three years by this time. The Berlin Wall fell two years before, in 1989. Now, returning all the Soviet states back to their former individual sovereignty was the demand. Four days previous to Mr. Gorbachev's resignation, eleven of the fifteen republics would secede and form the Commonwealth of Independent States

(CIS). Times were dicey, to say the least. And the day-to-day machinery of this vast land showed that things were in a state of disarray.

We waited two long hours to get our baggage, pass through customs, and find a taxi. We paid $6 to a private citizen to transport us and our luggage to the hotel. That driver made a killing. At ninety rubles per dollar on the official exchange, that one quick trip netted the man more than double the monthly salary of an average Soviet worker. And who knows how much he could exchange those dollars for on the active black market?

We had no reservations — there was no Travelocity or TripAdvisor.com back then, but thankfully, we found room at the inn. Khabarovsk was not an in-demand destination, and even getting a call through to that distant outpost was like trying to freeze helium — possible, but barely. We had traveled thousands of miles into a quickly deteriorating foreign country, not knowing for sure where we could stay once we got there.

It came as quite a surprise that this place didn't have the technology to accept credit cards, and their nightly rate was much higher than what Intourist had quoted me in DC. We ended up paying $88 cash for one night in a double room instead of the expected $62 on a credit card. Under normal circumstances, we'd each have had separate accommodations — Shotgunners rarely had to share rooms. *Oh, well,* I rationalized. *We're only going to be here tonight. We've got plenty of cash on us.*

You surely know what it means to assume ...

I was mostly oblivious to the signs of peril all around. My Mormon preparedness training should have been sounding a loud warning. Cash was king here, and hadn't I had enough experience in the Shotgun business by now to know that nothing in this country went as planned?

Our hotel was supposedly the best available. Its two-star

rating ranked it well above all others in town, which were listed as "primitive." As we lugged our belongings up the creaking stairway, we wondered where we'd find any signs of two stars! Opening the door to our room, a fierce cold immediately hit us in the face. Ice had formed inside the glass of the room's only small window. We each had a short, narrow bunk equipped with standard sheets and one not-so-thick blanket. I remember thinking, "I'd hate to see what 'primitive' looks like!"

"I've never been so cold," I muttered to Greenie through chattering teeth after we got settled. Even while wearing long John underwear and my heaviest coat and gloves, it didn't seem possible to get warm enough to sleep. There was pitiful little heat coming out of the radiator against the wall.

I couldn't handle it. I called down to the front desk.

"Can you please send someone to turn up the heat in our room?"

"Да. Give a few minutes."

No one ever came. It was too late to go out to find anything to eat, so we hunkered down for the night. I couldn't even bear to take off my boots, it was so cold.

"How can they call this a two-star hotel? There's no heat!" Greenie said as he stood across the room, stomping and blowing into his cupped hands. I wondered if we'd even survive the night.

"What are we going to do?" he asked. There were no better hotels, and we were extremely tired from our travels.

"I've heard survival stories where people had to combine their body heat to make it," I said.

Greenie had come to the same conclusion.

"Let's use both blankets and crawl into the same bed," he suggested.

I had already been married for almost fourteen years by then, and the thought of exchanging warmth with anyone but my dear wife was appalling. Now, however, there was no chance of getting any sleep unless we joined forces.

And so, for the first and only time in my adult life, I slept with another man. We avoided eye contact, both recognizing the awkwardness of the situation, and turned back-to-back. I flinched when his freezing toes, still draped in socks, brushed by my calf. He cringed when I accidentally elbowed him while adjusting my weight on the very narrow edge of the bed.

For a long time, I lay awake, teeth clanging in my head, as I listened to the wind howl outside that frozen window. After a while, I finally drifted off to an uneasy slumber.

Too soon, the effects of the extreme cold required a trip to the bathroom. Then it was back for another stretched-out effort to try again to settle into dreamland without actually touching my bed partner.

10 December 1991, Tuesday

We awoke early, eager to get out of that cramped billet.

"Let's get something to eat," I offered as soon as we were up, glad to have the uncomfortable night behind us. Maybe some warm *kasha* would help our bodies acclimate.

It was obvious that Brian was just as cold as I was. The only difference was that he had one of those black Russian fur caps with ear flaps that fold down from the crown as needed for warmth.

"That looks pretty comfortable. Where'd you get it?"

"I traded for it on a Shotgun trip. I now know why they're so popular here. They do a good job of keeping your head warm."

"Hmmm ... I'll have to try to find one. My noggin's so large, though, I wonder if they even make them big enough for me."

My dad's hat size was 6-7/8, which equates to a 21-5/8" diameter head. That's almost three full inches smaller than my enormous skull. Dad had discussed this extreme disparity with me in times past, both of us wondering how in the world his first-born son ended up with such a big dome. His theory was that my bones malformed during the birthing process. "Or maybe I'm just that much smarter than you," I teased. Whatever the reason, I'd always found it difficult to buy hats that fit. Now, more than ever, I needed a good Russian-style *ushanka*.

As we stepped out of the hotel, the frigid air caused a sharp pain in my lungs and I immediately felt the moisture in my nostrils crystallize.

I tried to spit to see if it would freeze before hitting the ground. It didn't, but that didn't stop me from complaining. "I'm not used to this kind of cold."

There was no response. Greenie was the strong, silent type. I wondered if he had even heard me. Maybe Siberia was the faraway land Greek philosopher Antisthenes spoke of where words freeze as they're spoken and can't be heard until they thaw in the summer!

We shopped but did not find a hat that would do anything more than balance warily atop my scalp. I bought it anyway — I had to have *something*! As long as I could pull the flaps down and tie them under my chin, I'd be able to keep it from falling off and at least stop my ear lobes from shattering like broken glass.

I also found a Soviet stamp collection for a little friend back home and a couple of unique clocks for $5 each that I thought would make splendid gifts. Who knew if they'd keep time?

It didn't cross my mind that I was spending precious cash.

The newspapers back home depicted long lines and shortages in the Soviet Union, but we saw just the opposite. We poked our heads into every shop and were pleasantly surprised to find no queues. True, food wasn't overly abundant and each place of business seemed to have a limited variety, but you could purchase onions in one store, cheese in another, and so on. Locals didn't seem to suffer from severe deprivations. We even found a nicely laid out jewelry case with five golden rings and a few brooches for sale.

I thought the news reports back in the States were a bit exaggerated, never considering that consumers were staying home, conserving their cash. Perhaps they sensed the impending doom of a country crashing around them. And who could enjoy shopping in this weather, anyway? The few people we encountered on the streets were bundled in layers of clothing, bracing against the cold with their faces barely visible. They were better dressed than I was to withstand the bitter temperature and the stiff, gusty winds.

We were back at the hotel by 1500L, packed and ready, but we found no messages giving us pickup details.

I called the Aeroflot station in town.

"What's the word on the charity flight coming through today?"

"*My nichego ne slyshali*," was the disappointing reply.

They'd heard *nothing*?

"Can you put us through to the Civil Aviation Ministry in Moscow?"

"No, we have no way to patch you through. You'll have to dial them direct." The phone call ended.

We felt like we were in the Wild West, dependent on the Pony Express to get information to and from the very powers that had asked us to make this churlish journey.

Telephones in Khabarovsk were extremely undependable, and long-distance calls had to be scheduled well in advance. We spent two full hours trying to get through to the Ministry, the people who had wanted us here so quickly, to find out what was going on.

Since no one accepted our credit card, we were fast running out of cash. We couldn't afford to just hang around waiting, especially with no word whatsoever.

Finally, we got through. "*Vash reys pribudet po raspisaniyu,*" they said.

"Wait, how could it still be on schedule? It's already two hours late! What time do you show it arriving in Khabarovsk?"

"*Vovremya,*" was all they could say. "On time." Worthless information after having worked so hard to get through to someone who should be in the know.

So we tried the US Embassy in Moscow. The phones were so bad, we finally had to give up, never connecting.

We had to go to bed for a second night in that freezing hole of a hotel, hoping against hope that somebody, somewhere, would get us word about what to expect. We didn't have enough cash to pay for a third night's lodging, even if we'd wanted it.

"Good night, Whick."

"Good night, Greenie. Sure glad I'm not here alone. It's good to have someone to suffer with!"

Chapter 21 - First Class and Evergreen

быть спасенным в последнюю минуту
"Saved by the bell"

World War II soldiers and marines came up with two very descriptive acronyms that fit this episode: SNAFU and FUBAR. If you don't know what they mean, look up their etymology. Both perfectly describe the situation Greenie and I were now in. If it weren't for divine intervention, things would have definitely degraded even further and we'd have probably frozen to death in a Siberian jail.

Two key deficiencies led to our almost-disaster: a lack of communication, and *mis*communication. What's the difference, you ask? Telephones didn't work well in that forbidden wasteland, and language and culture easily prevent understanding. It's as simple as that.

11 December 1991, Wednesday

Where we could pay in rubles, we made a killing. Breakfast on Tuesday was ₽5 each, the equivalent of 6¢ US. On Wednesday, the price went up to ₽7, a whopping 8¢. Tuesday night, we dined at the best restaurant in town, the Sapporo, a joint Japanese/Russian venture, for a total cost of ₽71, or approximately 75¢ for the two of us. The hotel tried to sell us souvenirs in dollars, but we could find the same things on the streets for rubles. Why pay $65 for a beautiful black lacquer box when we could get a similar one for $5 by walking a few blocks? Or $50 for a Gorby matryoshka doll that we bought in Moscow for $8 the month before? The same map of the town I bought for

1¢ in a downtown bookstore cost $3 in the hotel lobby. We contracted a taxi for $4/hour (which was way too much), but the hotel car cost $18/hour.

After we woke up on Wednesday, we went downstairs to pick up our passports, which were held at the front desk. Desperation grew when the receptionist mentioned we had received a call from a woman from the States, but since they had registered us under our first names rather than our surnames, the clerk had told her we weren't even registered there!

The State Department had never attempted to contact us during any previous Shotgun flight, but we surmised the caller must have been Becky Joyce, our State Department contact. Whatever she had to tell us must be extremely important; something about this particular mission was highly irregular. It was hard enough to make an outbound call from Khabarovsk; I imagine it was almost impossible to connect from afar.

We immediately tried to ring back but were told there was no way to get through to the States until 10 p.m., twelve hours later.

For our part, we still had no word from the Soviets as to the whereabouts of our flight out of that grim and cheerless place. It was obviously not coming, and we were nearly out of cash. The hotel refused to honor our secure, government-issued credit card to pay for a third night's stay, and there would be no commercial airline back to Anchorage until Sunday, if there was one at all.

What to do? The word "STRANDED" screamed in my head and landed flat on my soul.

Заброшенный (zabroshennyy) - abandoned, neglected, deserted, forlorn, godforsaken, jilted, cast aside, dumped and ditched. Woe unto the foreigners stuck in the nethermost reaches of a country falling apart!

We brainstormed ideas about how to get out of this mess, and our only escape appeared to be to take a twenty-hour train ride to Moscow, hoping to catch a flight home from there. We didn't have enough rubles to purchase the fare and we did not know if the rail station would even accept our credit card, but every option seemed like a gamble, and we weren't feeling any semblance of luck coming our way.

The receptionist could see that we were extremely miffed about missing such an important telephonic message, and she graciously rang Aeroflot and queried on our behalf.

"*Vash reys vyletayet segodnya* в *17:45*," she relayed as she held the phone receiver on her shoulder.

"Really?" I replied, our hope rekindled. If they actually planned for our flight to depart at 5:45 p.m. that night, all would be well. How she got that info perplexed us, though, since that same office had said the plane would be there "on time" on Tuesday and it never came at all. It also seemed strange that an ordinary hotel receptionist could extract the flight details we so desperately needed when we had spent half the previous day trying to get anything out of anybody!

We went upstairs and called the Aeroflot station ourselves. The connection went through, likely because it was just a local call, and we got the same response as the day before: "*My nichego ne slyshali.*" We have heard nothing.

Wow! Aeroflot, the scheduling enterprise for this entire fiasco, had no info. Yet the Civil Aviation Ministry had said that everything was as scheduled and the hotel receptionist indicated we'd be taking off at 5:45 that night. Total bewilderment. Had she made that up to keep us happy? Becky, back at the State Department, had something important to tell us but couldn't because they'd registered our names incorrectly. At once, all these conflicting messages amassed in a confusing pile of bright red flags. A deep-rooted survival instinct inside me squealed, "Get out of here! *NOW!*"

What if Becky from State had called because of some real emergency? Politically, things were in such an upheaval as to leave us wondering, with no reliable news available, whether we were in danger of truly being left behind, never again to escape the faltering USSR.

Adrenaline spurred me into action. I pushed Aeroflot harder.

"The hotel receptionist just said you told her our flight would be taking off at 5:45 p.m. tonight. Was she lying?"

Silence on the other end. Deep confusion filtered through the phone lines as this unidentified airline employee tried to make sense of what I was saying. I'm certain my shoddy Russian and her imperfect English collided and shattered any possibility of true communication.

"*Nyet*," she finally said. "We only show an Evergreen Airlines 747 coming through Khabarovsk at that time."

"Evergreen, the American LOGAIR company?" I asked incredulously.

"Да."

So the hotel gal had relayed a partial truth, and in doing so, she may have unknowingly given us our solution! There *was* a flight coming through at 1745L that night. It wasn't the flight we'd scrambled to escort, but it was headed the direction we desperately needed to go.

I thought back to Monday's flight, when we spoke to Bob about the new refueling venture for Evergreen Airlines they'd launched right here. Why hadn't it occurred to me to approach them before now?

Maybe we could hop back home with them! It was a long shot, but it seemed to be our only way out. Something had gone horribly wrong with the original plan, and either no one knew the truth or they weren't bold enough to tell us that we were stranded.

Still on the line, I asked the Aeroflot rep hopefully, "Do you know how we could contact the Evergreen station manager here in Khabarovsk?" By now, my heart was beating wildly, the full repercussions of not getting on Evergreen's Boeing 747 beginning to take shape as nightmares.

"Да, *konechno*." She gave me the number.

I dialed. It wasn't the right one. Darn! However, the man who answered knew someone who might be able to transfer us to Evergreen's local manager. He kindly passed along that person's contact info.

I called.

"*My amerikantsy, pytayemsya svyazat'sya s Evergreen Airlines. Vy znayete nomer telefona?*" I explained we were Americans trying to get a hold of Evergreen.

"Да, *konechno*." Exasperated, I wondered why everyone around there said, "Of course" so emphatically, as if they really knew something. So far, those words had proven completely hollow. At least this woman had access to yet another phone number.

I asked the operator to connect us for a third time. To my surprise, when the line connected, I heard the sweet sound of American English!

"Hello, this is David Bragdon."

"Oh, hi! Are we ever glad to hear your accent! This is Glenn Whicker, a Captain in the United States Air Force. Are you with Evergreen Airlines?" My voice cracked a bit, whether from the cold or the extreme anticipation, I couldn't say.

"Yes, Captain. I'm very surprised you found this phone number. We've only been here for the last five weeks, and we work out of a small, almost unfurnished office! What can I do for you?"

After explaining our unique situation, Mr. Bragdon gave

directions to his dinky workspace right on the airfield. We quickly gathered our bags and rushed to the airport. While awaiting our arrival, he sent a telex to find out what was going on with the Soviet escort flight we were supposed to have been on. Then he made a satellite phone call to their company's operations hub in Oregon to get permission for us to jump seat on their plane to Anchorage that evening.

As we walked in, huffing and puffing, he warmly greeted us.

"You guys were lucky to find me! We just got word that all Soviet flights were halted today due to the political turmoil in Moscow."

Greenie and I looked at each other, amazed that in one brief moment, he'd been able to clear up the extreme befuddlement we'd endured for several hours. Thank heavens for satellite communications!

The phone rang. He held up his hand to signal us to remain quiet while he listened intently.

His conversation lasted for quite a while, making Greenie and I nervous. The 747 was to land within the hour. What if they denied us passage? It was probably against company rules to onboard strangers. Airlines were governed by mountains of regulations, many of them imposed by international law. Maybe it would be impossible to cut through corporate red tape so quickly.

Finally, David hung up.

"I have both good news and bad," he began. "The bad news is that just two weeks ago, we had a couple of Boeing representatives who needed to hop a ride with us for similar reasons. Headquarters denied permission because they were not employees of Evergreen ... and, they did not have FAA flight credentials."

He could tell my sails were quickly deflating, so he hurriedly continued. "However, we do a lot of work with the Air Force[62] and you both have aeronautical ratings, so they said we could take you on!"

Brian and I both whooped with relief! We were going home, and in style.

We found out that Del Smith, Evergreen's founder, had a son, Michael, who flew F-15s for the Oregon Air National Guard. He had a soft spot for military flyboys! And it didn't hurt our cause that Mark, another of the CEO's sons, happened to be a passenger on this very flight. Every star aligned (finally) to create the perfect getaway scheme.

We awaited the Boeing 747 while glancing furtively at the thick cloud cover above us and to the south. We couldn't skip out of that town fast enough. When that gorgeous, warm, and inviting Big Bird, Jumbo Jet, Queen of the Skies, Whale of an aircraft eventually appeared in the distance, landing light gleaming as it gracefully descended through the clouds on its approach, I almost knelt in gratitude. Now, if we could be so lucky as to have no mechanical delays, we'd be on our merry way.

Because of Khabarovsk airport's archaic aviation services, it took nearly three hours to refuel the monster, a process that should have taken forty-five minutes. The crew had to pay $15,000 in cash because, once again, there were no credit card accommodations.

"How is this intermediate stop supposed to save the airline money?" I asked David incredulously.

He shrugged his shoulders. "I don't know, man. I just work here!"

---

62. Evergreen was under contractual agreement to augment the military airlift capability as part of the Civil Reserve Air Fleet (CRAF) should the need arise during a national emergency.

Then it hit me: David had accomplished an extraordinary feat in getting us out of there, but he was stuck in Siberia for who knew how long, a lone American single-handedly running his employer's business.

"You've been here five weeks already? What's it been like for you? What were your first impressions?"

He sighed. "When I arrived, I felt I'd settled on the far side of the moon amidst a junkyard of disabled Soviet planes. Our plane was on the ground for over three hours just to get fuel, and then I watched as it sailed off into the friendly skies to a familiar Anchorage without me. One of the loneliest feelings you can imagine!"

I felt for the guy. There I was, panicking after spending only two days in Khabarovsk, and he was there for the long haul.

"Anything I can do for you once we get back to the States?" I offered.

"Yeah. Call my wife and tell her I miss her."

While the preflight checks were underway, we scrambled onto the aircraft, tail # N471EV.[63] A quick look around astounded us — this was no ordinary 747. Evergreen did things with flair! Since theirs was a cargo-hauling operation, they didn't have to worry about catering to hundreds of needy passengers. We positioned ourselves in the luxury section just aft of the cockpit, relaxing in fully reclining overstuffed black leather lounge chairs. An exquisite kitchen stocked with every culinary delight imaginable was at our disposal, along with a commodious restroom and an opulent shower. We could watch TV, play movies, listen to music, and sleep comfortably in that cozy, spacious cabin.

---

63. This plane's sister aircraft, N-473EV, had been featured the year before in the blockbuster movie *Die Hard 2*.

We also had full access to the flight deck so we could revel in the beauty of such a nicely tricked-out aircraft.

The meals were excellent, and — may I mention? — the fully reclined chair-beds were warm! We were so comfortable, it felt like we were a floating castle in the air for the entire 2,500-mile trip to Anchorage.

We slipped away from Khabarovsk at 8 p.m. local on Wednesday and landed at 8 a.m. Anchorage time on that same day. Another time warp.

We could have thanked our generous hosts and purchased commercial tickets home from there, but by now, we'd made pretty good friends with our buddies who had extracted us from our dismal Siberian adventure. They seemed to enjoy our company just as much as we enjoyed theirs. After a three-hour layover on the ground at Anchorage, they invited us to stay aboard our extravagant airborne conveyance to make an additional 2,700 nm flight to Columbus, Ohio — another five and a half hours in pure luxury.

As we disembarked in Ohio, I shook everyone's hands and said, "Thanks again, guys, for helping us out. Your hospitality has been unbelievable." I gathered everyone's names and planned to find someone of foremost authority at the Pentagon to write Del Smith and tell him what an exceptional team he had.

"Wait, where are you going?" the pilot asked. "We'll be headed to JFK in just a bit. Won't that put you closer to your final destination?"

I was dumbfounded. I could be home in my own bed on the very same day I had thought I was doomed to the Gulag. Neither Greenie nor I could believe our good fortune.

12 December 1991, Thursday

The Boeing 747 had a hydraulic leak that had to be fixed on the ground at Columbus, so we didn't end up making it to JFK early enough in the evening to catch the last commercial flight to DC. But the appearance of this winged angel had blessed us, and I will never forget the smooth and comfortable ride we enjoyed from Siberia to New York aboard Evergreen Airlines' delightful Boeing 747-273C.

The 9:45 a.m. shuttle the next morning propelled us the rest of the way home, where I was reunited with my lovely wife and five young daughters.

The next morning's Washington Post[64] made it clear that my internal warning buzzers had been on the mark. Due to fuel shortages during the week, Aeroflot canceled all flights within the Soviet Far East. Ninety-two Soviet airports had already closed by Wednesday, and thirty-eight more were on the brink of closing, with Khabarovsk likely to be one of them. All forms of transportation had been disrupted, so even our desperate thought of taking a train into Moscow would have been untenable. The

---

64. https://tinyurl.com/WashPostSoviet

State Department had tried to notify us, and it was, indeed, Becky Joyce who had made that phone call.

Thankfully, the strong inkling I felt after learning of the State Department's failed attempt to reach us had spurred decisive action that prevented a potentially disastrous situation. Even if we'd had enough money to stay in the hotel until Sunday, the regular Aeroflot flight would have never materialized.

With up to 16,000 Soviet oil wells disabled, Greenie and I had been little pawns affected by a big international chess game: the destabilization of a once mighty superpower.

The bell of good fortune had indeed saved us.

Chapter 22 - Anadyr & The Bomber

Без труда́ не вытащишь и рыбку из пруда́

"Without effort, you cannot even pull
a fish out of the pond"

4 March 1992, Wednesday

This was destined to be a big one. We all knew that going in. Historic. Unprecedented. Unforeseen. For the first time, the most feared enemy bomber, the Soviet Tu-95 Bear, was to enter the United States — at our invitation! Not to bomb our cities, but to befriend the Russians in the new spirit of cooperation sought by both sides.

The Soviet Union was no more, and an inept drunk by the name of Boris Yeltsin led the recently independent Russia. He dabbled in what experts have referred to as *economic shock therapy*. The ruble exchange rate was no longer set by the regime, privatization of government-controlled entities flourished, and price controls were lifted. The progressive country needed to sell off its assets, and what better way than to showcase its military hardware to the only remaining world superpower, the United States of America?

In this new spirit of friendship, On March 4, 1992, two US B-52 Stratofortress[65] bombers flew to Dyagilevo Air Base near Ryazan, a Bear bomber training site a hundred miles southeast of Moscow. It must have been a sight to see.

Their new government required no military escorts to

---

65. Officially named Stratofortress, the B-52 is more commonly referred to as the "BUFF," for "Big Ugly Fat Fellow" (or a less polite version of that). The nickname reflects the aircraft's large size and distinctive appearance.

accompany our American crews on their flight over the Ukraine into Russia. Now, in a tit-for-tat exchange, the USAF had invited the Tu-95 "Bear" to come to the home of the B-52 "Buff" at Barksdale AFB, Louisiana, as an encore.

The only intercontinental bomber powered by turboprop engines, the Tu-95 is almost equivalent[66] to the B-52 in its capacity to inflict harm. It has an extremely long range (over 9,000 miles) and can operate at speeds only slightly slower than its turbojet competitors. An estimated 147 Bears were still in operation by 1992, while we still had about 170 Buffs in operation.

The question was: Could we allow them to fly across the US from the West with no escorts? After all, they hadn't imposed their in-flight chaperones on our visit to their base. But if we put Shotgun pilots aboard, Americans would get our first up-close look at the Bear in action.

3 April 1992, Friday

My boss, Al Westrom, and I went to a meeting at headquarters to discuss the exchange scheduled for May. The Russians understandably didn't want us on board. The powers that be at the Pentagon, namely HQ USAF/XO[67], the operations guys, sincerely wanted to provide them the same courtesy they'd afforded our crews during our visit to their base.

The FAA, however, probably under pressure from the State Department, insisted we put escorts on because our airspace is so

---

66. For an interesting video comparing the two competing bombers, see https://tinyurl.com/CompareB-52
67. XO was the office symbol for the Plans & Operations Directorate of Headquarters, United States Air Force, Pentagon.

much more congested than theirs. Since Al and I were just innocent minions in this big power play, we had to sit quietly to see how it all panned out.

29 April 1992, Wednesday

More than three weeks passed before we got the final word. The bomber exchange flights would use us as escorts, after all. Westrom, Greenie, and I suddenly needed to be in Moscow by the weekend. I'd never been on a Shotgun trip with my boss before, so this was to be a real treat.

1 May 1992, Friday

May Day, as celebrated in the Former Soviet Union, honors the working class. Because of that, they couldn't issue visas until Monday. Getting visas for each individual Shotgun trip is a giant hassle. We needed multiple-entry visas to go along with our blanket orders, but that was never going to happen.

Our commercial flight to Moscow was scheduled to depart at 1855L Monday evening, so the timeline was really squeezing us. After landing, we would have a full day in Moscow followed by a seven-hour, 3,300 nm Aeroflot flight to Anadyr, a port town on the northeast coast, just across the Bering Sea from Alaska.

Because of their superior language abilities, Brian and Al would each fly in one of the two Bears, and I'd be in the AN-124 support aircraft. No American had ever been on board their bombers in flight, nor had this ominous enemy aircraft entered the US. Yes, they'd played cat-and-mouse games with us by flying along our coast, just outside our national airspace, but that was a totally legit Cold War game. To have one actually penetrate the Continental United States was headline-grabbing!

4 May 1992, Monday

Getting our visas was difficult. I imagine the officials in charge received guidance to play hardball in response to our government's uncompromising requirement that we be on board.

The Russian Embassy is a gorgeous edifice completed in 1985. It sits just off Embassy Row in Washington, DC, and includes a residential building, a school, and a sports complex for diplomats and their families. The consulate is completely separate. We visited it often and knew Nikolai well. He usually treated us cordially and gave us priority based on our Shotgun mission.

This trip, Nikolai tried to mess with us. "Your request doesn't show the dates and times of arrival in Moscow. Go back to the State Department for a better letter!"

"Nikolai, we couldn't do this on Friday because you were closed for May Day. Our flight leaves tonight, and we don't have much time."

"You know I can't give you a visa without those details! I promise it'll only take ten minutes when you get back. Go!"

And so I left, certain there was no way to complete the round trip before they shut down for a leisurely lunch hour at 1230L. Despite that, I rushed to Becky Joyce's office and explained our dilemma. Thank goodness she was at her desk! She quickly threw in the needed details, then printed and signed the freshly edited letter.

It was 1215L by the time I made it back. The queue was way too long, full of business people needing visas, but after waiting a few minutes, I remembered: We had diplomatic passports now — I didn't have to wait in line! I immediately passed all those neatly dressed men. They looked at me with disdain. Who did I think I was, butting ahead of them like that?

I ignored them, turned in the required correspondence, and sat down to wait.

At 1230L, everyone was told to return after lunch, but I stayed.

By 1245L, no one was left in the office, and still there was no word. In desperation, I walked up to the caged window.

"Nikolai, I need those three visas for our trip tonight!"

Again, he played the headstrong gatekeeper. "Everyone's at lunch. Come back at 3:00."

We had a taxi scheduled to pick us up at 1630L from Ft. Belvoir, but I had no choice. I left wondering how I could possibly be back at 1500L and make it to our pick up on time.

To kill time, I drove the twelve miles to Bolling AFB, where I got a haircut. Then I remembered we'd need some trinkets to trade with our foreign counterparts, so I ran over to the BX to make some purchases.

When I returned (for the third time ...), Nikolai thought he'd given me the run-around long enough. The visas were ready.

As fast as one can in heavy Washington, DC, rush hour traffic, I drove to the Det and had exactly one half hour to pull everything else together before we were out the door.

Pam brought the girls by to say goodbye as, in my mad rush, I had missed seeing them off to school that morning. After hugs and kisses, I promised each daughter I'd bring them something nice from Russia. That was the only way I knew to make up for my week-long absence.

The three of us — the boss, Greenie, and I — were scheduled to fly to Frankfurt, but wouldn't you know it — Germany closed its borders that day due to nationwide strikes. Just another of the hurdles we had to overcome in this crazy job. We exchanged our tickets on the spot and flew to Paris instead. Thank goodness for blanket orders that allowed immediate flexibility. The mission must go on!

5 May 1992, Tuesday

Air France got us to Moscow, but changing our flight at the last minute had thrown a wrench in their system and they lost our luggage! They said they knew where my bag was, but they couldn't find Westrom's or Greenie's at all.

A taxi took us to the Slavjanskaya Hotel, where we hoped to be reunited with our personal belongings.

6 May 1992, Wednesday

Still waiting for our bags, we did some shopping. The remnants of the old Soviet way of life were novel enough to me that finding unique gifts to take home was enthralling.

While Westrom returned to the hotel to receive the found bags (thank goodness!), Brian and I made a quick trip to the famous Arbat Street, where I bought a really nice matryoshka doll for $8 and a gorgeous $27 black lacquer box for my wife, along with some cheaper boxes and brooches for my daughters. The taxi back to the hotel was fifty rubles, which, at an exchange rate of 115 rubles for a dollar, equaled 44 cents.

Our flight out of Moscow left the Domodedovo Airport in the southern part of the city at 1700L, so we arranged for a pickup at 1300L. The taxi was waiting at the hotel right on time, and we enjoyed the long drive to an airport that only Al had ever seen before. Along the way, we passed some famous landmarks, such as the Novodevichy Convent and Moscow State University. I vowed to return someday to explore the monastery more closely, but that opportunity has never arisen.

Flying as commercial passengers across the breadth of this vast country in an IL-62 operated by Aeroflot was quite comfortable, though long. The seven-hour flight included a very nice in-flight meal, complete with caviar. I was brave and tried it again, but the little pustules tasted like salt water when they burst in my mouth! I do not understand why people consider them such a delicacy.

7 May 1992, Thursday

We crossed nine of the eleven time zones of the Former Soviet Union to land at Ugolny Airport (UHMA), across the Anadyr River from a town of the same name. In effect, we lost sixteen hours, landing at 0900L Kamchatka Time (PETT). Built in the 1950s as a "bounce aerodrome" for long-range bombers, the field serves as a joint civil-military airport. Supposedly, twenty Sukhoi Su-15 Flagons were based there in early 1992, but none were on the ramp during our visit. The interceptor squadron had likely already disbanded by then.

Anadyr is the easternmost town in the Russian Far East, although there are a few other small settlements that don't achieve the status of a town. It is a port where the Anadyr River empties into the Bering Sea. There is no easy way across the river from the military base, so we never saw the actual town of Anadyr. In the summer, one would have to take a boat to reach the city proper, and in the winter, they use an ice road. However, during the spring thaws while we were there, you could only make the jump by helicopter, because there was no bridge.[68]

The Base Commander, Colonel Niparko, picked us up and drove us out to the military side on extremely rough dirt roads. Honestly, even as a relatively young man, I remember how careful I had to be to keep my back straight as we bounced into

---

68. In October 2021, a three-year project was announced that would build an air-cable bridge across the estuary between the airport and the town.

Capt. Whicker at flight briefing

and out of giant puddle-filled potholes. I became concerned over the health of my jolted bones!

They served us a very nice breakfast of fried potatoes, apple juice, mystery meat, and cottage cheese with some sort of sauce. It was a very decent meal.

Although better than the hotel Greenie and I had shared in Khabarovsk, the quarters we stayed in here were pretty austere. The toilet had no seat. I slept on a futon in the living room for a too-long nap, arising only in time for an expansive four-hour meal with the Commander, his "political officer," and a helicopter pilot. Westrom and Greenie each drank several glasses of what they described as rather good cognac, while I sat back as a teetotaler, absorbing with fascination my two compadres' ability to carry on long and detailed conversations in this difficult foreign tongue.

I felt like such an imposter; I had less than a three-year-old's vocabulary and yet I had been selected to undertake this important mission. Although I captured parts of the overall gist of the

Greenie briefing Russian crew

conversation, I couldn't join in because of my poor language skills.

As was the case everywhere we went, these people were extremely gracious. They gave each of us a matryoshka doll and a nice little carved box. It was an enjoyable evening.

8 May 1992, Friday

It snowed a bit, but it was the wind that made things so blasted unbearable. We went out to the airport to greet the AN-124[69] and the two Tu-95 crews coming in from an eleven-hour flight from north of Baku in Azerbaijan.

Kostya, our jeep driver, backed into another vehicle. He was a funny-looking kid; not a single hair on his head was combed! Most of the people, however, were quite impressive and went out of their way to treat us well.

All the navigators and radio operators met with us to brief

---

69. https://tinyurl.com/IntroAN-124

Victory Day festivities in Anadyr

Saturday's long flight to Barksdale AFB, Louisiana. Greenie did a superb job of speaking with everyone to ensure they were all aware of what was to be expected once we hit United States airspace.

9 May 1992, Saturday

Victory Day! Considered the most important of all national holidays, May 9th[70] celebrates the end of The Great Patriotic War (1941-1945).

Russian celebrations of triumph over Nazi Germany dwarf those of any other Allied force by far to remind the world of the tremendous contributions of the Soviet Union in winning that conflict. They have good reason for their pride in such an

---

70. In the US and Europe, VE Day (Victory in Europe) is celebrated on May 8. Since the exact time at which all hostilities were to cease was 11:00 p.m. Central European Time, it was already May 9 in most of the Soviet Union.

accomplishment; they claim that their country inflicted almost 90% of all combat losses suffered by the Nazis, and their numbers certainly back up that statistic — nearly 27 million Soviet citizens lost their lives in the war. Compare that with 420,000 American deaths, and 450,000 from the United Kingdom. Theirs was a monumental effort, and all of humanity should honor that extreme sacrifice.

While thousands of troops paraded through Red Square in Moscow, this little Anadyr base staged its own impressive show of military prowess. A parade, a speech, a mock battle, and good food and fellowship made the day memorable. The barbecue, *kasha* (buckwheat), shish kabob, and black bread were all superb — the best meal of the entire visit.

Our hosts eagerly showcased their country's achievements to us Americans. I wasn't prepared for the spectacle of it all, but throughout the proceedings, you could feel a vibrant sense of pride. It was refreshing to see, especially against the backdrop of such bleak buildings, cold weather, and barren terrain.

As special guests, we got a lot of attention. I felt a warmness, a closeness of sorts, to these people. Many wanted photos of themselves with the "Amerikantsi." My specialty was the dozens of little children enjoying the show. They came up to hear a bit of spoken English. I asked how old they were, how many siblings they had, etc. A few even tried their spotty English on me. Intrigued by my oh-so-foreign accent, they'd ask what time it was so they could hear my horrible attempts at Russian. Then they'd laugh heartily! I didn't care. I knew how bad my language was!

They all hoped to snag a coin or a piece of gum or candy, but I didn't have enough to go around and unfortunately left many disappointed after word spread that I'd passed out a few little tidbits. Kids quickly overran me and I had to pull back a bit.

Everyone opened up to us. Kostya, our jeep driver asked a lot of questions about the States. One little boy made a special effort to retrieve a spent ammo cartridge from the mock battle to give me. It touched my heart. Having been a young lad myself, I recognized that such a find would be extremely meaningful in his personal treasure trove. His eagerness to share demonstrated a delightful disposition.

They were all good, kind human beings. That day, my perception of the Former Soviet Union elevated a notch.

After all the festivities, Westrom and Greenie got into a billiards tournament with some of the local crewmen while I watched, completely perplexed at the unfamiliar rules they were using. Their version of the game is called Russian Pyramid, and I'd be hard-pressed to explain how it works. All fifteen numbered balls are white, while the cue ball is red. The balls are slightly larger than Western pool balls, and interestingly enough, the pockets are narrower. Such an arrangement makes the play extremely challenging. It was entertaining to watch.

After that came the most heart-warming part of the experience. About two hours before we were to leave our room to get out to the airplanes, a steady stream of visitors dropped by with gifts. The level of generosity was incredible! The helicopter pilot we had shared dinner with the first night brought not one, but three 2-foot salmon, smoked, salted, and individually wrapped several times in brown paper. Goodness! I immediately wondered how in the world we'd get them through US customs. But the gesture was genuine.

The airfield manager gifted us each a little chunk of rosewood root — a very simple offering, but something he cherished. He said it acted as an aphrodisiac if you let it soak in your vodka for twelve days. I've never been able to prove his claim one way or the other. I just took his word for it.

Colonel Niparko, who had already given us plenty the night before, presented the group with a gorgeous set of reindeer antlers mounted on a beautiful wood background, along with a bottle of champagne. In turn, we gave him a bottle of California wine, and a Book of Mormon in Russian (what a combo!) Westrom still has that magnificent rack hanging on his study wall.

We had the privilege of meeting the Colonel's family in their small apartment right next to our room. They were the most lovely people. His wife, true to the nature of any woman anywhere in the world, apologized profusely for the untidy state of their abode. She was so humble and cute. The family's gratitude at being able to host us was unforgettable.

Finally, our driver, Kostya, showed up at our door with a bag full of homemade cookies and jam from Galina, the server at the officer's mess where we dined while on base. We walked over to thank her, and as Colonel Westrom graciously explained to her how much we'd enjoyed her cooking, her eyes welled up with tears. It was enough to make me want to hug her as I would my own mother. She shyly asked to have her picture taken with us. Where was all this love coming from?

At 1500L, Kostya came back to take us to the airfield, where we received the flight brief in the company of the crews of all three aircraft. The General Major of Aviation, Anatoliy Soloviev, gave the briefing. This was the first time I ever heard a complete flight briefing in a foreign tongue, and it was hard to follow. My profound language inadequacy bit at my soul with an unrelenting sting once again.

As we left the meeting, I asked for a toilet and was told that this large, supposedly well-equipped training building did not have a restroom. I would have to "hold cargo."

Despite the warmth and love I felt for the people who had

shown us so much kindness, my wonder at their crazy system of priorities rose again.

We went directly to the airplanes. Before boarding, the bomber crews, with their Shotgun escorts, proceeded to the grass under the tails of their parked planes to urinate ... *in formation.*

Chapter 23 - The Bear 'N the Buff

Быть не в своей тарелке
"To be out of one's own element"

9 May 1992, Saturday (continued)

Flying in formation requires extreme discipline. The lead aircraft has to be smooth and predictable for the others to follow. The lead pilot must expand his awareness to a larger bubble than just the area surrounding his own airplane and consider timing while giving his wingmen adequate signals to react to the lead. The wingman's job is to 'be there,' supporting the lead.

Although ours was a very loose formation, separated by a mile instead of mere inches, as in an aerial demonstration team, these same factors apply. Aircraft numbers 2 and 3, in this case, were the two antiquated Bear Bombers. And I do mean antiquated, as will soon become blatantly obvious.

Blazing the trail in the large and much more modern AN-124, the crew I escorted were the main communicators with controllers, in whose minds, we three were one entity. A single directive was meant for all, but only aircraft #1 needed to reply. The implication is that if the lead acknowledges, all understand and will comply.

The Bears were to loyally follow our every move, including frequency changes. Talking on radios quickly becomes second nature to pilots, and the unique language of aviation comes easy after a while. There are both written and unwritten dos and don'ts when transmitting. It isn't hard to get on the bad side of ATC if you lack proper radio etiquette.

One major rule is to be quick and precise. A single air traffic controller can handle up to twenty-five planes simultaneously, so they frown on any delay in responses or any misunderstanding that results in a need for repetition.

"Handoffs," where ATC passes an aircraft onto an adjoining air sector controlled by a separate entity, are common and can be frequent when transiting busy airspace. If you are sent to a different frequency, you should check in with the new guy expeditiously.

On this historic flight, radios became a significant issue.

Departing Anadyr in the Far East of the Former Soviet Union, we didn't have to talk to anyone for the first hour or so. As we approached the area marked by the light blue dashed line on the map below, we were required to contact Anchorage Alaska's Air Route Traffic Control Center (ARTCC). It has responsibility for two and a half million square miles of airspace, much of it oceanic.

The Russian crew's aeronautical publications had some bogus frequencies listed for Anchorage Center, so it took us far too long to do our obligatory radio check-in. I finally stepped up and, by reference to our US charts, found the right contact. By then, we were almost to St. Paul Island, halfway through Anchorage's airspace. I was totally uncomfortable with that, but

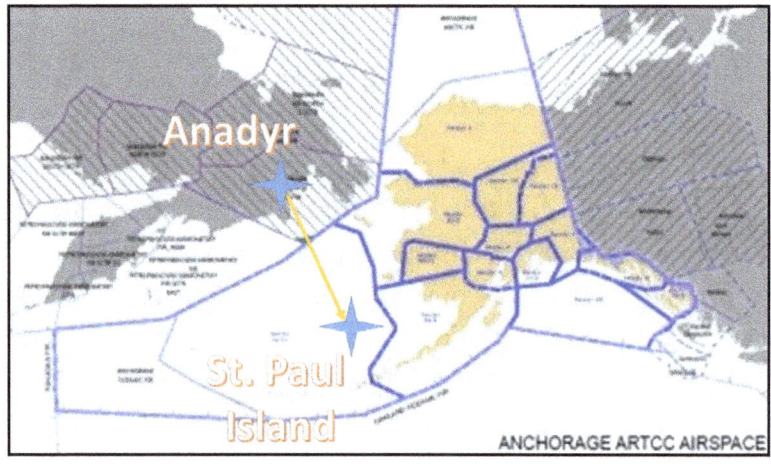

we did everything we could to correct the situation.

No one seemed to have missed us. We were flying over the open sea, so there was no real chance of a traffic conflict anyway. We were initially cleared for a block altitude from 21,000 feet up to 23,000 feet, which is pretty low for a long-distance jaunt. The higher you go, the better the fuel efficiency, so I'm not sure why we stayed down in those regions for so long.

When flying in formation, a flexible 2,000-foot vertical block is preferable to a hard altitude assignment because it allows the aircraft to separate from each other by a safe distance. Wingmen can then position themselves below or above the lead aircraft to keep him in sight without the physical and mental exertion needed to stay in a tighter formation.

Approaching Seattle, they climbed us to a block of 25,000–27,000 feet MSL and shortly thereafter offered a further increase of 2,000 additional feet. These were much more comfortable altitudes for these jets.

As we entered the Continental US (CONUS), radio changes came much more often than they had ocean-side. The lead AN-124 could easily keep up with the frequency changes using our modern radios, so moving from one sector to another gave the crew no challenge. But somewhere over Montana, Westrom called me up on the inter-plane frequency and clued me in on a serious problem.

"Glenn, I don't know if you've figured it out," (I hadn't), "but the radio system we're dealing with in these old bombers is horrendous! It takes us at least two minutes to make each frequency change. Could you please check us three or four minutes after every new station to make sure we're still with ya?"

I should have been doing that anyway. Still, it was surprising! I couldn't imagine how a routine change from one frequency to

Flying the Condor

Almost all my flight experience was in relatively small, single-piloted jets. Working with a multi-person crew was alien to me to begin with, and flying a "Heavy" aircraft such as the AN-124 was a completely new experience! The UK Civil Aviation Authority even classifies the Ruslan (Condor is NATO's name for it) as a "Super-Heavy" aircraft.

Our job as Shotgun escorts was not to physically pilot the Soviet planes. We were merely extra crew members on board to ensure safety and compliance. However, on 9 May 1992, Colonel Razoumenkov, Commander of the AN-124, took a liking to me. He let me hand-fly it (no autopilot) for about twenty minutes during our descent into Barksdale so I could get a real feel of how it handled.

I made slight turns and minute changes in our descent rate, just to experience the aircraft's superb in-flight characteristics. Its size and weight made it quite stable, even in choppy air. As Colonel Razoumenkov configured the plane for landing, he gave me the real shock of the day.

"You've got the landing!"

The landing? Was he saying he wanted *me* to land this, the sister of the world's largest airplane, when my whole aviation experience was in much, much smaller aircraft? I couldn't believe my ears, but I

Tech Tab #9

jumped at the chance. Of course, he was right there, totally in control in the same way I'd been as a flight instructor during thousands of student landings.

After trimming the flight controls for the approach speed, I was amazed at its sturdiness. It wasn't so susceptible to turbulence or winds as the U-2 or T-38 I had so many hours in, and the response to control inputs was instantaneous, unlike the delayed response common to some large airplanes.

The landing was superb! I can't swear to it because I was concentrating so hard, but I never saw the Captain make any physical corrections other than reducing the power for the touchdown. He talked me through the landing flare, which was very needed. The sight picture of landing from a cockpit a full four stories high was completely different from my usual experience seated a mere four feet off the ground.

The greatest part of the whole deal was that he signed a Soviet logbook for me, calling me a "First Class Leader-Pilot" and giving me undue credit for two landings and four ILS approaches! Good times!

Glenn at the controls of the AN-124; looks like a mighty SHARP right turn!

the next could take that long! Expeditious use of a radio is one of the earliest lessons a pilot learns in training. Whatever challenges they were experiencing behind us in the antique bombers were beyond my comprehension, having never seen the relics they had to work with.

I knew there must be a good reason for his request. From that point on, I made doubly sure they were properly sent to each new frequency. I made a courtesy radio transmission a few minutes after the changeover to ensure they were with us on the new freq. Even so, we would encounter serious issues during the approach into Barksdale AFB.

I later learned that the main radio in their bombers was limited to five preset UHF frequencies that the Bears used all the time at their home station. To change to a frequency other than one that had been set on the ground before takeoff, the radio operator had to go through quite an unusual dance:

First, unscrew four Dzus-type fasteners, then physically remove the 5" x 5" x 5" radio head from its perch inside the instrument panel, and flip it upside-down to reveal its back side.

Perform mathematical calculations to convert to modern UHF frequencies from their archaic system. Only then could the five new digits be dialed in one by one on little turnstiles that you might find on an old combination lock. With a ball-point pen, rotate the tiny cogwheels into the active position. Finally, carefully replace the entire radio into the panel, ensuring each sprocket locks into place to make the proper electrical connection. Now a transmission can be made or received on the new frequency.

It took forever to accomplish what should have been a simple feat. Was it set up that way so that it would not be easy for a crew to dial up 243.0, the US emergency Guard[71] frequency, and say, "We want to defect?" Or was the Soviet system just that technologically complicated back when the aircraft was manufactured in 1956? Who knows? My dad flew even older B-25s and B-29s as a flight engineer, and I can assure you our radios in the 1940s had annotated dials to make frequency changes simpler.

The lack of multiple radios on those old tin cans also meant they could only speak on one frequency at a time: VHF, HF, or UHF. Since their government demanded the bomber crews make periodic reports back to Moscow on HF, the Tu-95 was out of touch with our formation and the ground controllers for long periods.

We in the lead aircraft were completely unaware they weren't with us on frequency during those absences. Luckily, while

---

71. Pilots, air traffic controllers, and military personnel are expected to monitor (or "guard") the emergency frequency at all times. This ensures that any aircraft in distress can quickly reach help. Guard is a protected channel that is kept clear of interference to ensure reliable emergency communication.

cruising at altitude, wingmen didn't necessarily need to hear every direction given to the formation as long as they kept us, their lead, in sight at all times and we had inter-plane communication.

Eventually, though, our formation would have to break up, as each aircraft would have to be handled separately in the terminal phase of our flight approaching Barksdale.

I have no idea why our more sophisticated AN-124 wasn't making those required HF reports to Moscow, as it would have saved so much grief on the part of the bombers. Perhaps no one thought of that when the mission was briefed back in Anadyr. Or maybe, though I can't imagine this being the case, it was because the homeland powers were much more concerned about losing one of their valuable strategic bombers than they were about the Antonov.

Brian and Al were making history as the first American servicemen to actually fly inside a Soviet bomber, but they were so frustrated! Not only were the radios a bugaboo to handle, but apparently the entire aircraft stunk to high heaven because of the lack of facilities at the Anadyr airport before our departure! I guess the Soviet technology of the 1950s didn't offer the Tu-95 an adequate plumbing system.

As the Shotgunner in the lead aircraft, I certainly didn't help my buddies as much as I could have. Had I been more fully aware of the machinations they had to go through each time we changed frequencies, I would have been more deliberate about confirming that they were successful at making each adjustment.

Al later reported that at one point over the Northern Tier, they were on the wrong frequency for over an hour!

That complexity caused big problems on the approach. Descending into congested airspace, we lost the flexibility of a block of altitudes and had to drop our identity as a formation.

Pages from the Soviet Pilot Logbook gifted to Glenn
by Major General A. Soloviev, Vice Commander, Long Range Aviation
(giving me far too much credit!)

Now each of the three aircraft were solo, and had to be handled individually by ATC. When a Bear was sent over Arrival Control's frequency, the crew got bogged down with the change and didn't respond to heading and altitude directives in a timely fashion. This made it so other aircraft in the area had to break out of the sequenced pattern as our friendly Soviet bomber continued on an old heading for miles after it was told to turn.

Once again, a torrent of humiliation coursed through me, coloring my thoughts with a deep, unshakable crimson as I listened helplessly to the floundering over the radios.

In the end, we all landed safely.

Once we were down, I had the chance to go up into one of the Bear's cockpits and see how crazy the radio setup was and how it all worked. I was truly amazed at the complexity of what had always been such a normal, easy process for us.

This visit was a big deal, helping to break the icy tension of the Cold War. Prior to landing, the bombers made a low approach, then pulled up to come around again to land. The distinctive purr of the Tu-95 was created by the unusual configuration of their eight-bladed counter-rotating props. Onlookers found it eerie to hear that unfamiliar sound in the skies above, and when they looked up, they were even more startled to see a big red star on the tails of the planes.

Soviet Bears & US B-52 together on the ramp at Barksdale AFB

The Russians got a royal reception at Barksdale, complete with a rousing military brass band. Crowds of military personnel and civilians waved US flags and the new flag for the Commonwealth of Independent States (CIS), which had come into existence after the dissolution of the USSR less than six months before.

"I never thought I'd be awakened by a call from command post saying, 'There are two Russian Bears over Oklahoma City and they're heading your way,' and still be happy," said Brigadier General George P. Cole, Jr., commander of the largest bomb wing in Strategic Air Command at Barksdale AFB.

For well over four and a half decades, America had lived with the constant concern that these foreign, antiquated bombers would appear in our skies with malicious intent. During those years, hundreds of airmen sat on alert pads around the clock at strategic bases across the country, poised to run to their ready-cocked B-52s at the sound of a warning klaxon. By regulation, they had just fifteen minutes to have their plane rolling.

Those alert procedures continued until just eight months before this historic exchange.

Now, that long-term enemy finally arrived, not as aggressors, but as ambassadors of the new CIS republics. Those same American aircrews who were positioned to counter a Soviet attack were now mingling excitedly with their would-be attackers on the ramp of a United States Air Force Base.

"I think both groups have been longing to know each other for a very long time, but for various reasons, that wasn't possible," said Lieutenant General Martin J. Ryan, Jr., commander of the 8th Air Force.[72]

---

72. You can see the Airman Magazine article on this historic visit here: http://u.pc.cd/x377

We spent the night in the Ramada Inn next to the airport and had a nice Louisiana dinner at a fantastic restaurant. We got up early to catch an 0630L flight to DC. A layover in Atlanta kept us from getting home till after noon, though, so I missed church with my family. My truck was at the Det, so Al's wife Judy picked us up and took us all to our office. I stayed for an hour to make preliminary phone calls to line people up for the return trip with the bombers, as we decided we should let three other Shotgunners handle the return to spread the wealth.

Chapter 24 - Boris Meets Stone

*Лучше один раз увидеть,
чем сто раз услышать*

"It's better to see once
than to hear a hundred times"

"With this agreement, the nuclear nightmare recedes more and more for ourselves, for our children and for our grandchildren."
- George H. W. Bush

10 June 1992, Wednesday

"I can't make it," Schweitzer said.
"Why?" I asked.
"Car troubles."
Once again, one of my Shotgun escorts abandoned me, and I had to take on a high-profile mission myself at the last minute.
Senate Minority Leader Robert J. Dole had invited the new Russian president, Boris Yeltsin, to Kansas to see the home base of the B-1 Lancer bomber, witness for himself the efficiency of mid-America's wheat farms, and tour a meat-packing plant.
From the opening days of 1992, the big dog in Moscow was Boris Yeltsin. Despite Yeltsin's prolific reputation as a boozer, he had enough political chutzpah to deftly position himself to take the reins as soon as Mikhail Gorbachev stepped into the sunset of history in December — on Christmas Day, in fact.
Now his glamour session with the President of the free world, George H. W. Bush, was on the horizon. Yeltsin desperately wanted to build on the magnificent strides in arms reduction initiated by his famous and popular predecessor. The planned summit could provide him just the vehicle to do that by

expanding the reductions settled upon with the START 1 treaty.[73]

To prepare for a deal as big as Yeltsin's trip to the United States, most militaries worldwide send an advance party to scope out the places their VIP will visit. It looked like I was going to be escorting an IL-76 from Andrews AFB in Maryland to McConnell AFB in Kansas so his team could look at the airfield ramp and see where they'd be parking the next week with their president on board. The plan was to get in and out of McConnell as quickly as possible. We would only be on the ground for ninety minutes, and the flight itself was an hour and a half each way.

I was less than enthusiastic about escorting this humdrum ADVON[74] team a week before the main man himself was to arrive. It was mundane and routine, and it meant spending a whole day on an assignment I'd expected someone else to handle. Things like this continually popped up, making my personal life impossible to schedule.

11 June 1992, Thursday

This was the most rapid paced day of my entire Air Force career. Greenie and I had no fewer than eight missions to coordinate, all in connection with President Yeltsin's visit the next week. We had to find crews, make travel arrangements for the Shotgunners, interface with the FAA and State Department to provide appropriate routing for each flight, and give the Pentagon a summary of each mission. If that wasn't enough, a high-priority last-minute problem came up with two Russian Su-27s trying to get to an airshow in Portland, Oregon! Sheesh!

---

73. The first of two eventual Strategic Arms Reduction Treaties
74. A military ADVance echelON party sent to scope out a location prior to arrival of the main contingent.

That took some time to iron out.

I also had to finish preparations for Lt. Colonel Westrom's Change-of-Command ceremony the next day. We all loved and respected this fine leader, and it was sad to see him move on.

When I got home, I quickly mowed the front lawn, rushed to Tara's band concert at the middle school, and packed while trying to help Pam with a baby that wasn't feeling well. Sometimes the pressures of life can almost squash you!

12 June 1992, Friday

Greenie met me at the squadron to participate in welcoming our new boss, Colonel Phelps. In the military, all authority and responsibility rest in the hands of a commanding officer. No organization may be without a designated commander, even for a brief period. A ceremonial handover of the unit's flag makes it abundantly clear to all who is in charge. The instant the incoming commander received the guidon[75] from Lt. Colonel Westrom, he proclaimed, "I assume command," and all the weight of leadership transferred immediately. It's a nice way to order things. I've always appreciated the precision of the military way of life.

There was no time for social pleasantries after the formal proceedings; Greenie and I sped to the Russian Embassy in downtown DC to get our visas for the trip, then headed straight to Reagan International Airport.

For the coming summit, an IL-62 Classic would transport President Yeltsin non-stop from Moscow to Washington, DC. Because there were no intermediate stops, Greenie and I were

---

75. A guidon is a small flag carried by a military unit as an organizational marker. It represents the unit and its commanding officer.

required to board in Moscow, the point of embarkation.

After an uneventful trip over the Atlantic, we made our way to the Sheraton Palace Hotel in downtown Moscow.

13 & 14 June 1992, Saturday & Sunday

We did some shopping on Saturday. A store near the airport sold small Russian lacquer boxes for $425 each! They really are beautiful, but we knew we'd find some just as nice for our wives at much lower street prices. The exchange rate at the hotel was only ₽90 per dollar, but we found an American scientist who offered us ₽100, so we each bought $300 worth of rubles from him. Later, on the street, we found the black market rate was ₽140! When we ran out of rubles, we found a store displaying the VISA logo and tried to buy a charming box using our credit cards. But it was all a ruse — they wouldn't accept them! This effort to morph from communism to

A table of matryoshka dolls for sale on the famous Arbat Street in Moscow

capitalism was proving a difficult transition!

On Sunday, we visited a couple of local churches. A taxi drove us to the address we had for the Church of Jesus Christ of Latter-day Saints, but the lady there said the Mormons hadn't met there for quite a while. The first Latter-day Saint unit had only existed for two years. So we found two Russian Orthodox chapels and enjoyed looking around inside each one. The aroma of incense smacked us squarely across the face as we entered, and the chapels themselves were ornate and full of paintings, icons, candles, statues, and golden crosses. On the walls, frescoes depicted biblical scenes in vibrant colors on a gold background. Gold, glitter, and jewels were so predominant that unless you saw the little old ladies reverently paying tribute to their Lord, you would not have known these were places of worship.

Greenie and I were both genuinely touched by the sincerity of the women's devotion. These were those whose faith had kept the churches open during the oppressive decades of communism. The *babushkas'* consistent reverence for God made possible the religious resurgence of the early 1990s that caused some of the airmen we flew with to sometimes wonder about the divine.

We spent the evening preparing for the next day's big flight and made contact with the people transporting us to the presidential aircraft the next day. It would be one of the longest Shotgun flights I ever made — a pretty significant ten-hour hop across the Atlantic. Our Shotgun duties, however, only required us to be in the cockpit for the last couple of hours.

15 June 1992, Monday

There were three aircraft in this contingent, flying a loose trail formation. Since we'd only be over US territory for a short distance, the lead aircraft, with Yeltsin aboard, was the only one of the three requiring escorts. Once we moved on to McConnell AFB after the main event, penetrating farther into the homeland, all three aircraft would need onboard escorts. For now, the other two planes would simply follow behind in our bubble of cleared airspace.

As Greenie and I climbed the steps and entered Yeltsin's posh IL-62, we were escorted to the first-class cabin, forward of the deluxe suite provided for the Russian President and his entourage. Unfortunately, we didn't get to meet Yeltsin in person. He entered the aircraft through a rear door and never came up to greet us. Despite that disappointment, it was going to be a great flight, with ultra-comfortable seating, highly delectable dining, and no real duties until the very end of the flight. With such a high-profile VIP along, we wore our Class A Air Force blues, the official dress uniform, rather than our normal flight suit "green bags."

The sharp uniforms caught someone's eye.

While awaiting engine start at Vnukovo Airport, Greenie sat at the window and I was by the aisle to accommodate my longer legs. Suddenly, I was startled to have a 12" camera lens shoved into my face, a mere hand-width from the tip of my nose! A bright light blinded me, as the person behind the camera loudly exclaimed, with a full, deep voice, "The US Air Force? We didn't expect to see you here. What are you doing aboard the Russian president's plane?"

I recognized the voice immediately. It was none other than Stone Phillips, the famed hard-hitting news journalist from NBC's award-winning Dateline program. He was there to interview President Boris Yeltsin during this historic flight to Washington DC, and either he or one of his production crew had noticed us getting on the plane — we stuck out like sore thumbs in our military regalia. Before Phillips got down to business with the real and pre-planned subject of his interrogations, he pounced on us. A shining target of opportunity was impossible for him to ignore. His famous "tell-all" personality beamed at the prospect of revealing to the world the heretofore unheralded requirement for our presence on Yeltsin's plane. Our quiet little Shotgun program was suddenly going public on national TV! There was no way out.

Scan this code to see Stone Phillips's report or go to: tinyurl.com/YeltsinShotgun

At that point in my career, I had not received any media training that senior military officers are offered regarding public relations, specifically on how to handle reporters and journalists — not that it would have done me much good in this instance. I was so flustered by the unexpected intrusion into my personal space and by the big, obtrusive camera and its associated lights and booming voice using perfect English that my reaction would probably have been just the same.

I whimpered.

In a blubbering, unintelligible attempt at a response, I basically said nothing. My tongue got out in front of my brain, and to my surprise, gushed forth in complete idiotic nonsense!

Thankfully, while I sniveled meaningless grunts, Greenie had a few seconds to gather his composure. When Stone finally gave up on my worthless reply to his query, he shoved the microphone toward my companion and had the camera focus on him. Calmer and more collected by then, Greenie delivered a somewhat intelligent, sensible, and understandable answer to Mr. Phillips's reasonable, but abrupt, question.

When the episode aired the next night on prime-time television, it was Greenie's more measured response the world heard, as the news crew had graciously cut out all of my recondite mumblings. I only showed up on the broadcast performing my later duties on the radio in the cockpit. I will always be better as an extra on film than as a primary actor. Still, if everyone's life includes fifteen minutes of fame, I suppose this was our fifteen seconds!

Greenie responded to the Dateline host: "We're here, basically, to ensure that the airplane gets to Andrews and so that, as Glenn says, they understand our air traffic control system and they don't miss any clearances. We're kind of the last guarantee of safety. And we speak a little bit of Russian, so that's why we do this."

The truly big news that emerged from Dateline's presence on the aircraft came during Phillips's interview with President Yeltsin. Among other highly diplomatic subjects discussed, Boris dropped a political bombshell by suggesting that the Soviet Union had imprisoned US servicemen captured in Vietnam during our long-past conflict in Asia. He even suggested that some might yet be alive!

No one saw that bolt from the blue coming. Was he being serious, or was he drunk? Was this a problem with translation? That unpopular war had disappeared from world news over twenty years before, and now a world leader was suggesting there were still American POWs living in Russia. Whoa!

The special presidential envoy to Vietnam for POW/MIAs, retired Army General John W. Vessey, Jr., declared that it "does not square with what we thought we knew. It's absolutely new information."[76]

President Yeltsin also said that Soviet prisons and psychiatric hospitals had kept twelve Americans shot down in the 1950s on

---

76. https://tinyurl.com/NoRussianPOWs

spy missions. This piece of intelligence seemed a bit more plausible. Important documents were soon to be released to the public, disclosing that the USAF had lost several men during secret RB-47 overflights during that decade. The disposition of those airmen was unknown.

As a recent reconnaissance pilot, I found all of this extremely interesting. My last U-2 flight had been in December 1990 during the build-up to the First Gulf War, and I'd heard that the Secretary of the Air Force's Declassification Office had already run across some materials on the subject of the lost RB-47 spy planes. It would take time to delve into that mystery sufficiently to learn the fate of those aircrews. My mind whirled at the possibility some of those airmen had survived and become prisoners within the Soviet Union, just as Francis Gary Powers had been after the infamous U-2 incident of 1960.[77]

Such revelations from the Russian President prompted a flurry of activity, with US President Bush sending envoys to Russia to uncover more details. Within just a couple of days, it turned out that Yeltsin's POW claims from the Korean and Vietnam conflicts were unsubstantiated. His chief authority on the subject tried to cover for his boss by saying that he had been talking only in "possibilities," and that, "There is not a single fact or case that is known to us."[78]

Yeltsin's aircrew, by the way, was the finest I ever flew with. They knew their procedures, spoke excellent English, and didn't need us. It was a pleasure to have an unremarkable, safe Shotgun flight. I barely felt the aircraft touch down upon landing, it was so smooth! Just like our Air Force One captains, these pilots were surely the best in their country, hand-picked to fly their

---

77. For more on this, refer to https://tinyurl.com/SpyPilotsKilled
78. Retired Gen. Dmitri Volkogonov, https://tinyurl.com/YeltsinClaimFalse

 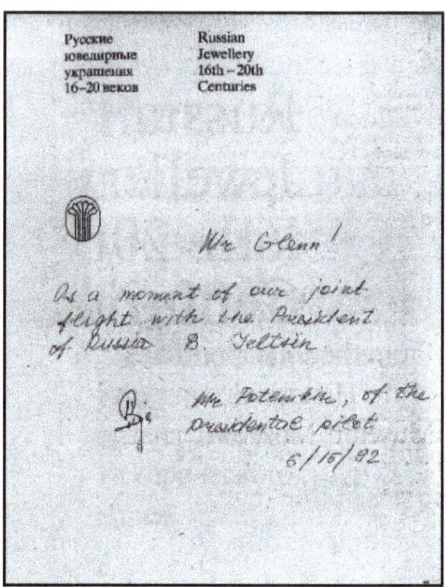

The cover and a note written inside Pilot Potemkin's gift to Glenn

head of state. The chief pilot, Mr. Potemkin, signed and gave Greenie and I each a book of Russian paintings — an extremely thoughtful gesture.

Once we landed, we watched from our window perch as Yeltsin greeted US Secretary of State James Baker.

Both sides proclaimed the summit a success, with further reductions of nuclear arsenals agreed upon, billions of US dollars promised to enhance Russian economic reform, and a definitive end to the Cold War declared.

Postscript: 19 June 1992, Friday

Remember the quick flight I escorted to McConnell AFB I made nine days before the flight with Yeltsin? It had helped set the stage for Yeltsin's only US stop outside of Washington, DC, after the summit. The irony of the Kansas destination was not lost on many.

His IL-62 and two accompanying IL-76s landed near Wichita at the invitation of future presidential candidate, Robert "Bob" Dole. Not only was this the location of the strategic B-1B nuclear bomber poised to pounce on the USSR during the Cold War, but before 1986, it had also been home to the organization that controlled eighteen Titan II missile silos, each armed with the largest single warhead of any American ICBM. Both of these weapon systems were designed specifically to counter any threat posed by the former Soviet Union, and here stood the new leader of the remnants of that powerful enemy nation.

Conclusion

Всё хорошо, что хорошо кончается
"All's well that ends well"

I am proud of my thirty-six years of service to my country. I was only paying back a small portion of what the United States of America has afforded me and my family.

It was quite a thrill to ride Shotgun in the sidecar of history. You can hear world news and get a distant perspective, but to see it happening up close and personal gives you a wholly different outlook.

Constant Shotgun taught me that we are not so different from the people of the USSR. A Soviet military officer had the same dreams, aspirations, loves, and fears I had. Like me, he looked to provide for his family and offered his allegiance and service to the country he loved. He wore a uniform daily, as I did. He wondered, deep within his soul, about God and his own purpose in life, as do we all. Those I met loved aviation, rejoicing in the beauty and freedom of flight, just like me.

How can you hate a brother?

Ours is an awesome country; in fact, the Book of Mormon calls the Americas a "choice land ... above all other lands." It took me many years and many more miles to finally realize that America's true strength lies not in the pride we occasionally display, but in the values and resilience that unite us. In fact, false pride is a weakness that needs to be stripped from our common psyche, for we are of no greater worth than any other people living on this Earth.

The grandeur of our land isn't rooted in its beauty or natural resources, though we are greatly blessed in those respects. Other lands have their equivalents to national parks, Rocky Mountains, and Niagara Falls, and others have deep oil reserves and large strains of precious metals waiting to be mined.

It isn't in our riches. Though we are blessed with an extremely high standard of living, living like a king does not save us in the end.

Nor can the greatness of this nation be attributed to its powerful military. I've had the privilege of flying some of the most sophisticated aircraft in the world, steeped with good old US technological ingenuity. But I've also been able to fly several Soviet aircraft and witness their engineering. They are strong, and their military training is of a high quality.

No, the distinction that makes our land choice above all other lands is our ability to lift and serve others among the family of humanity who are not so blessed. Our form of government was inspired from on high, and in that lies strength. It was not created to lift us in pride and arrogance, but rather to provide a stable platform from which the greatest blessings available can flow as honey to the world.

Instead of hoarding the beneficence allotted us, let's look for ways to promote the building up of others, understanding that they, too, have families they love and dreams they aspire to.

Russians and Arabs and Chinese are God's children too. We don't have to accept their political ideologies to comprehend their intrinsic value as human beings. Our founding principles value life, and war is only justified to free the oppressed or maintain the freedoms of those blessed with it. We uphold the values of America "in memory of our God, our religion, and freedom, and our peace, our wives, and our children" and in anticipation of those same values for all.

Yes, America is great because America is good.

Appendix

Друзья — это те, кто всегда рядом
"Friends are those who are always near"

The following entries were provided by fellow Shotgunners. I thank all who participated in Constant Shotgun, especially those who provided this further documentation of the historical program.

ONE: FIRST FLIGHTS
Lieutenant Colonel Al Westrom, USAF (Ret.)

I had been an Assistant Air Attaché in Moscow from July 1985 to July 1987. Prior to that, I was a B-52 instructor pilot and I really wanted to get back into flying after being out of the cockpit from 1983, as I went through extensive academic and language training for the attaché assignment. I learned of an assignment in the Washington, DC, area that was a flying billet. It was unclear as to what kind of flying I would be doing, but what was clear was that a part of my job would be flying as an on-board escort for Soviet "special" flights. I applied and was accepted and reported to Ft. Belvoir, Virginia, in August 1987.

Once there, I found that there were two flying slots, the other occupied by Major Pete Shockey, who took me under his wing and explained that we had an informal agreement with Det 1, DCANG[79] at Andrews AFB to fly their C-21 Learjets. He also explained that our escort duties tended to be for the twice-a-year flights bringing in and taking back the Soviet, Ukrainian, and

---

79. Washington DC Air National Guard

Belorussian delegates and families to the United Nations.

My first Constant Shotgun trip was one of the last "standard" flights. Twice a year, the Soviets flew their UN staffs (including Belorussia and Ukraine) in and out. Up until that time, these UN shuttles had been the vast majority of diplomatic flights, and therefore the limit of Constant Shotgun.

Major Pete Shockey worked for Det 21 as an assistant ops officer and was the senior Shotgun pilot. He had flown KC-135s in the Air Force and learned his Russian at the Academy. Pete took me in hand and showed me the process.

Before the flight, we had gone to the basement of the Pentagon to the Air Force Operations Center. We actually carried diplomatic passports (I just kept mine from Moscow with the approval of State). At the Pentagon, we received Pentagon passes and, more importantly, parking permits! Nobody there could really give us a good briefing on what they wanted or needed from us, except to say that we needed to contact them inbound and outbound on each flight and they would handle communications for us.

So armed with our parking passes, we set off for Gander, Newfoundland.

Gander is a desolate city, somewhat centrally located on the island of Newfoundland. It is on a very broad, beautiful river that gives the impression of being a fjord. But the entire island is a cold, boggy place with little topography. One of the many things making Newfoundland unique is that they not only are on their own time zone, but it is thirty minutes off from the rest of the world.

At the time, we stayed at the Aladdin, a hotel also used by the Cubana Airlines crews. They were a swarthy-looking group, always hanging about in the halls with their doors open and seeming to be partying. We imagined they were cooking goats in their rooms from the pungent smells emanating from therein.

Pete walked me through the routine of getting past Canadian customs and meeting the RCMP[80] officers there. The Aeroflot flights were handled by one of the FBOs in the terminal, so we didn't have to deal with the Aeroflot offices. Nice people there, with an AUTOVON line because they handled so many DoD flights.

I actually don't remember much about that first flight. Pete did the work; I watched. The cockpit of an IL-62 is large enough to accommodate two additional people, so we weren't really in the way. Pete had told me to keep an eye on the navigator and that he would work with the radio operator. The navigator was annoyed to have me watching, and I had no idea how his systems worked (one was Omega; another, inertial) or where we were, so I was useless to this effort. In fact, in all my many flights, I never did figure out how to tell where we were except by dialing in a ground-based navigation system, VOR, and watching the needles.

Our flight to JFK was empty and uneventful. We went to the diplomatic parking area to the NW of the field and waited for the baggage and people to board. Pete and I went to the Pan Am dispatch section, where we coordinated the filing of the flight plan. Basically, we didn't want the Soviets overflying the submarine base at Groton or the SAC base at Loring. A standard departure and flight to Gander or over the Atlantic would normally avoid both.

Our standard procedure was to be in the cockpit whenever over US airspace. Normally, this was a point called DAVES intersection. Inbound, we would ask the radio operator to allow us to use the HF to call and get a phone patch with USAF Ops Center and tell them that the Constant Shotgun pilot was on

---

80. Royal Canadian Mounted Police

board prior to DAVES inbound. Theoretically, if that call wasn't received, the flight would not be permitted to proceed. But we found that if we couldn't get through, no one at New York Center seemed to care.

On this trip, at DAVES outbound with the UN delegates and staff on board, Pete and I went to the front cabin where two seats were reserved for us. I was pleased to find that we had not missed cocktails. In fact, the stewardess was making the second round (about forty-five minutes after takeoff). She had a cart with ice, glasses, and large liquor bottles. I asked for Scotch and got a large tumblerful. Little did I know that even the diplomats attending the UN would be unaffected by the Gorbachev effort to curb alcohol consumption in the Soviet Union. This would be the last glass of Scotch courtesy of the Ministry of Foreign Affairs for me. But that situation was in the future and out of my sphere of concern. Aided by a glassful of good Scotch, I slept most of the way to Shannon, my first mission complete without a crisis.

For some reason, Pete Shockey was unavailable for an unusual trip. We were to meet the Soviet airplane in Montreal and escort it to Washington. Since this was an abnormal flight routing, State wanted escorts on board. I believe that we were escorting a delegation visiting Canada and the US. Since we always traveled in pairs and Pete wasn't going to be with me, I invited Lt. Col. Dick Unser, my predecessor in Moscow, to accompany me on the trip, which looked like a good one.

This was the first time that Dick and I had spent any serious time together, and we spent an evening in Montreal swapping Moscow stories. At that time, Dick was working for DIA, responsible for all their air operations, which consisted of numerous C-12 turboprop aircraft at various embassies around the world. So Dick was a pilot, current, and knew enough Russian to be effective. I don't remember much about the flight, which means it was most likely uneventful.

However, our next one included a few interesting moments.

I believe Dick and I went to Gander to escort the UN delegation back to the US. This time, we decided to visit our Canadian comrades at the Canadian military outpost near the Gander airport. The Canadians were more than happy to see us in their tiny officer's club and fed us steaks and beer. We subsequently got a group together to go into town, where a two-person band was playing at the Hilton. We drank, had a good time, danced with some of the local wives, and went back to our hotel past the Cubana crews partying late into the night at the Aladdin Hotel.

The flight into JFK presented us with our first situation where the Aeroflot pilots would not listen to our advice. We were cleared for a complicated instrument/visual approach to a short (8,000 foot) runway. The approach flies over the Canarsie VOR, then flies a radial of the VOR to the north while descending. Soon, you pick up a series of bright, sequenced strobe lights on the tops of buildings that bring you in a gentle arc around to land on runway 13 Left which means the arc takes you from north through southeast.

First, we missed our mandatory crossing altitude at Canarsie. This was a crew mistake because they expected to be given altitude crossings by the controller, but in the US, when the controller clears you for an approach, you are responsible for all altitude restrictions published on the approach. I could not convince them to descend, so we crossed Canarsie some 1,500 feet high. I simply notified the controller. This meant that our descent was going to be steeper. We got down to our recommended altitudes on time, but because of the increased descent rate and looking for the runway (which is hard to see even in good weather), our airspeed was high. I thought the pilot was going to land on runway 13 Right because most of 13 Left was hidden by airport buildings and structures. When he finally saw 13 Left, we were in a fairly unstable approach. The pilot never lost his excess airspeed, which caused the aircraft to float a bit. When we finally touched down, he really had to stomp on the brakes to slow down for taxi.

After taxiing a bit, the radio operator told Pan Am ops that we might have hot brakes and to have a fire truck standing by when we parked. As soon as we did park, the engineer ran off the aircraft and got the fire truck to pull closer to the landing gear. I got off after him to watch while customs cleared the passengers before letting them off of the airplane and onto the busses.

Just as the head passengers were coming down the stairs at the front of the Ilyushin, the engineer put a fire hose into a hole on the main landing gear wheel and turned on the water. A huge plume of steam enveloped everyone on the stairs and lasted for several minutes. Although I didn't see it, Dick told me that he later saw the old engineer with his arm around the shoulder of the young pilot telling him not to worry, it could happen to anyone. The pilot was obviously concerned about possibly losing his international flying privileges.

We stopped in Gander again on the outbound leg. We were tired but wanted to visit a few of the bars our friends had told us about. We arrived about 8:00 p.m., but the bars were absolutely dead. Then, around 10:00 p.m., business picked up until 1:00 a.m., when they shut down. It seems that Newfoundland, being a commercial fishing dominated area, was in the midst of a serious recession. Many of the locals were on welfare. Since they didn't work, most hit the bars at about 10:00 and went home and slept until mid-morning, then started all over again.

TWO: EMERGENCY COMMUNICATION
Lieutenant Colonel Al Westrom, USAF (Ret.)

During the 1970s through the early 1990s, there were a series of "special" flights between the US and the USSR. Some were routine, such as transporting the Soviet, Ukrainian, and Belorussian delegations to and from the UN in New York, as well as flights in support of the US Ambassador in Moscow (usually to and from Rhein-Main AB). Some were not so routine, such as a flight from JFK to PHL to aid in the filming of Rocky V. And there were a series of earthquake relief flights from LAX in support of the Armenian earthquake in 1988.

For several reasons, the United States Air Force placed Russian-speaking crew members on these fights when inside US airspace. The most compelling reason was that the Soviet government required that any USAF aircraft entering the Soviet Union must have a Soviet navigator and radio operator. These flights, during my experience, were mostly in support of the ambassador on a passenger-configured C-9 from the 55th Wing at Rhein-Main AFB.

Additionally, there were infrequent congressional visits (CODELs) on board 89th Wing VC-135s or VC-137s from Andrews AFB. We tended to express our displeasure at having to have two Soviet aircrew on board by demanding "reciprocity" of having two USAF crew on their flights.

A former B-52 and C/T-39 instructor pilot, I had been an Assistant Air Attaché in Moscow from 1985-1987 and had participated in many ambassadorial flights (he was authorized six round trips a year) that were used to great effect to fly in fresh fruits and vegetables as well as toilet paper. We also hosted several CODELs.

But as President Gorbachev's programs of *glasnost* and

perestroika became more solid, there was a planned, but rapid, growth in diplomatic flights that culminated during my Moscow tenure with a multi-plane visit by US Secretary of State Shultz. By that time, we had become experts in Moscow airport operations (both Sheremetyevo and Vnukovo), which meant we knew how to get things done and where to find help. This reached its peak when we had to emergency medevac an 89th Wing crew member on an Air Force C-21 positioned at Sheremetyevo in the middle of the night. Within six hours of the embassy doctor recommending him going to the Wiesbaden Hospital, we had gotten the crew from their hotel, obtained diplomatic flight clearance, and transported him to the airport. I shocked the KGB border patrol guards by pounding on the sleeping room door of the KGB Major in charge of security, and after he got mostly dressed, had our guy airborne within another fifteen minutes. (Interestingly, the C-21 was there in case Secretary Shultz had needed to send a secure message to President Reagan. At the time, there were concerns that the Soviets had breached our security and the C-21 was to be a messenger plane if needed!)

After leaving Moscow, I was used by the Constant Shotgun program as an onboard escort for Soviet diplomatic flights. This consisted of biannual UN flights to and from JFK on Aeroflot. Basically, normal Aeroflot international crews did an extra flight segment and were highly experienced in flying to and from JFK. Rather than using the normal Pan Am gate, these "special" flights usually parked in a different area. That presented a problem on one flight when our empty plane was taxiing in and the captain insisted on going to his normal gate. This caught me by surprise (as we had briefed just a few minutes earlier about the special area), and my Russian failed me. I told him to "turn left, TURN LEFT" in Russian and then tried to add, "believe me!"

but the imperative of that verb is non-standard. When the crew heard me yell "Boil me!", they stopped, looked at me, started to laugh, and then turned left.

In 1987, Lt. Colonel Dick Unser and I were contacted by State Department to leave for Prague immediately for a diplomatic flight. We arrived on Lufthansa in the morning and were on an evening flight for Andrews AFB on board a special IL-62 with Foreign Minister Shevardnadze. This was the preparation for the Gorbachev summit in Washington in December. This flight was uneventful, but it was obvious that although some of the crew were experienced Aeroflot international flyers, some were not.

Our responsibilities were fairly simple. We positioned ourselves in the cockpits for any flight operations over US airspace. Inbound, we used the Soviet HF radio to make an inbound call to USAF Operations Center informing them we were aboard. We tried to assist with explaining procedures at airfields the Soviet crews were not familiar with. Many times, we inserted ourselves on the radios to facilitate communications. In my case, at least, my Russian was adequate, but less than I wanted. We always traveled in pairs.

When word came down from State Department about the proposed Gorbachev summit in Washington, DC, we learned that there would be four aircraft in the official party: three IL-62s and one IL-76. This fleet was to depart Brize-Norton RAF base, fly non-stop to Andrews AFB, and return, several days later, non-stop to Schönefeld Airport in East Berlin.

We in the Constant Shotgun program contacted all the Russian linguist crew members we could to form four teams of two. We arrived at Brize-Norton a day early and were well taken care of by our RAF comrades, although several of us complained of the lack of showers in the Officers' Mess, bathtubs being preferred in the RAF culture.

I assigned myself and my predecessor in Moscow, Lt. Colonel Dick Unser, to the primary aircraft, that flying President Gorbachev. The compartment immediately aft of the forward entry door was primarily for the president's staff. It included typists, security guards (who were very suspicious of us), lower level support staff, and Dick and myself. We were welcomed by the crew but not the commander, who was waiting for his president at an aft entry door. We were seated in the comfortable front cabin of the IL-62 during taxi-out. I was in the aisle seat when I heard a very strange noise. It sounded like a kid making machine gun noises with his tongue, and when I turned around, I saw Gorbachev's personal bodyguard next to the window, holding a large revolver and pointing it at the RAF VC-10s and L-1011s out the window, making the machine gun noises. When he saw me looking at him, he scowled but put his gun away.

Dick and I were fairly tired from the previous evening's preflight events with the rest of the Constant Shotgun team and fell off to sleep fairly quickly. I was shortly awoken by one of the flight crew asking me to come to the cockpit. Dick and I had introduced ourselves to them already, so it was odd to be asked to come forward. When I did, still a bit groggy from the short nap, the radio operator handed me a headset with a very perplexed look on his face. He also handed me a pad of paper and a pencil. Listening to the air traffic controller, instead of standard ground-to-air communication, I heard a rambling statement. Soon it was clear I was hearing a message for President Gorbachev, in English, and it was beyond the capabilities of our radio operator to transcribe. So I started writing, and, at the end, had Shanwick Oceanic Control repeat the first few paragraphs from the Irish Prime Minister, wishing Gorbachev well and success on this crucial meeting for the entire world.

I wrote it up, received extreme gratitude from the radio operator, and then went back to the cabin where the translator did his thing and the typist, hers. I had to do this once more when we were in Canadian airspace, and this time was ready for the message from the Canadian Prime Minister. But as we were only an hour or so from US airspace, I stayed in the cockpit.

Dick joined me as we flew over DAVES, the first inbound US point. The cockpit was very professionally run by Captain Maiorov. We really didn't have much to do, but as in all other Constant Shotgun flights, we were standing throughout the flight, to include approach and landing. It was not uncommon for others to join us for a total of ten or so in the cockpit during critical phases of flight!

No arrival issues presented themselves for us to be useful, so we just watched the spectacle unfold. A huge crowd was there for us, including President and Mrs. Reagan. After President Gorbachev deplaned, Dick and I stood in the forward entry door and watched as he was greeted and made a speech. It was a spectacular event, and our participation was captured in a photo on the front page of the Washington Post. I'm the one in the light vest in the doorway (we always traveled in civilian clothes).

The summit was a success, and we prepared for the departure with the same teams on the same aircraft. It was a cloudy, somewhat rainy day, and the departures out of Andrews were a series of directs to various fixes, some on Victor Airways, some on jet routes, so there are a lot of turns at low altitude on these departures. We briefed the navigator on these. He used lat/long manual entry into his system, which provided course guidance on the pilot's equivalent of an HSI. Everything went flawlessly until we were about 3,000 feet AGL. Someone burst into the crowded cockpit and spit out something in excited Russian that neither Dick nor I could understand. Then Captain Maiorov got

Gorbachev arriving at Washington Summit, with Al Westrom on stairs

out of his seat and started to leave the cockpit! But before doing so, he leaned over to the radio operator and discussed something with him. Then the navigator handed him a comb.

He fixed his hair and then left the cockpit. I was very focused on his empty seat as we passed 3,500 AGL, wondering what I should do. My concern was somewhat ameliorated by his attention to his hair, so Dick and I looked at each other and wondered, "How bad could it be?"

After a couple of minutes, our captain returned and we learned what had happened. One of the more senior members of the president's party had gotten in the wrong SUV and did not make our flight. President Gorbachev noticed that there was an empty seat in his section and wanted the captain to personally deal with it. We radioed back to the other planes that they needed to find the wayward passenger and find a place for him on another aircraft. The cockpit crew was fairly amused that one of the big cheese communist leaders couldn't even get on the right aircraft.

It was a great flight to East Germany. Unlike the inbound trip, our mission was over and we allowed ourselves some excellent liquor being poured into large glasses for us, without mixer of course, by the very nice stewardess. We fed off of the good moods of the Soviet entourage. When we landed at Schönefeld airport in East Berlin, there was a moderately sized crowd greeting Mr. Gorbachev, but they were not terribly warm toward him. In fact, when we were being driven to West Berlin, it was fairly obvious watching the departing crowd that they were just happy to have been excused from work for a few hours and were throwing away the factory made signs that they had been holding.

West Berlin was ready for Christmas, and Dick and I enjoyed their outdoor markets, toy stores, carolers, and hospitality. We had been lucky enough to witness history from a front row seat and luckier still to be back in the West.

THREE: HELICOPTER BABUSHKAS
Kenneth E. Todorov, Brig. Gen., USAF (Ret.)

In the summer of 1992, I was serving as a pilot and, at the time, Executive Officer to the Wing Commander at Det 3 of the Air Force Flight Test Center when out of the blue, the personnel officer in the wing called me to tell me there had been an inquiry about my availability to serve on a special mission. While there were few details provided, he was able to tell me that it involved helicopters and the use of my (limited) skills in Russian. I was provided a number to call at (I believe) WPAFB[81] where I could get more information. Being intrigued, I followed up on the lead.

When I established contact, I was told that my skills were needed to help escort a group of two Russian helicopters who were making some sort of goodwill mission from Moscow to Miami. The Shotgun program was explained to me in broad terms, and I immediately asked my O-6 boss to support. After some reluctance (who would push paper in the Wing, after all), my boss, Col. Bill Dobbs, agreed that I could support.

The mission was to take place in October 1992. I was to meet the Russian crews and their MI-8 Hip and MI-24 Hind in North Dakota. I would help them through US airspace, assist on the radio, ensure the crews were bedded down each night, and generally keep the crews out of trouble. Seemed easy enough. It turned out to be a real adventure!

The trip was aided by a number of sponsors including the US State Department, the Milbrooke company, and the Whirly-Girls association of women pilots.

I would soon learn upon arrival to North Dakota that the main crew was a duo of women led by Galina Rastorguyeva, a

---

81. Wright-Patterson Air Force Base, Ohio

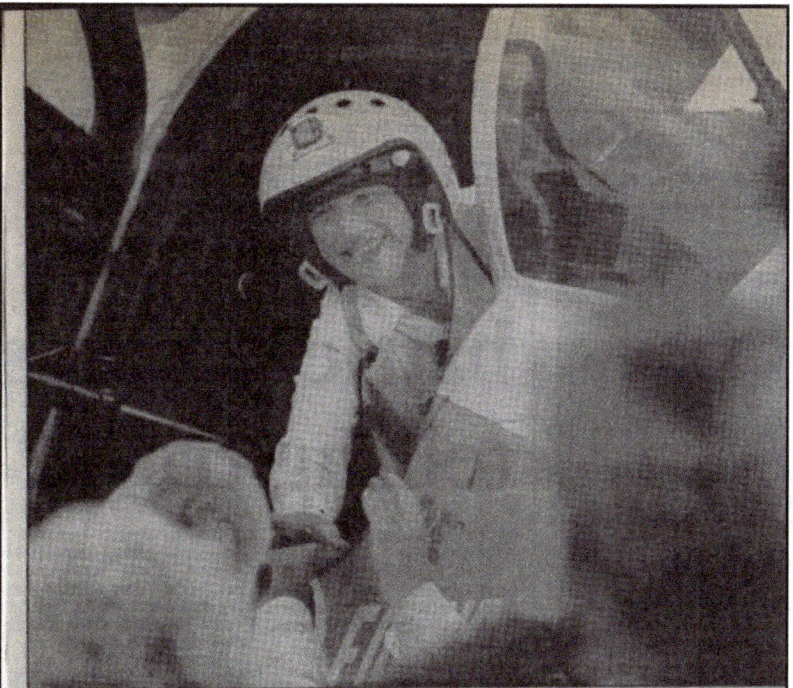

PATRICK FARRELL / Miami Herald Staff

WARM WELCOME: Galina Rastorguyeva is greeted by well-wishers Monday as she lands on Watson Island. She and a countrywoman flew two choppers from Russia in a 41-day trek.

Women pilots soar into Miami

By DAVID HANCOCK
Herald Staff Writer

From Moscow to Miami in 41 days.

Russian helicopter pilots Galina Rastorguyeva and Ludmila Polyanskaya saw lots of territory while flying two Soviet-made choppers through Siberia, Alaska, Canada, North Dakota, Iowa, Missouri, Alabama and Florida.

And you know what most impressed the two women in their aerial view of the United States?

"They're amazed at how neatly the roads and buildings are laid out — the little cottages, the planned streets," said translator Larisa Ignatieva.

Rastorguyeva and Polyanskaya added a Russian flavor to Columbus Day events here. They ended their three-country trek on schedule Monday at Miami's Watson Island. The two women were the only ones of the 10-member Russian crew to fly the two choppers.

Their trip, which was made in four-hour jumps for refueling, was aided by a grab-bag of sponsors — including the U.S. State Department; the Milbrooke company, which is bringing a Christopher Columbus statue to Miami Beach; the Whirly-Girls association of women pilots, and others.

Rastorguyeva, a 56-year-old grandmother, is one of Russia's pioneer women test pilots. Monday, she pointed proudly at a number of her speed records painted on the side of the red-white-and-blue Mi-24 combat chopper. Polyanskaya, 54, a career navigator, followed in a Mi-17 cargo chopper.

Rastorguyeva said the Russian government has donated the choppers to be sold in Canada for a cause dear to her heart — a planned "resort" for women pilots in Moscow.

seasoned veteran female test pilot, age fifty-six, and a grandmother. She had been some sort of pioneer of Russian rotary wing aviation fame. Her cohort, a much younger Ludmila Polyanskaya, also a pilot/navigator, was primarily the maintenance officer for the mission. Accompanying the women was a cadre of Russian Army pilots and "political officers" who would watch over the women. Most prominent was Major Alexi Minayev, a combat-proven MI-24 test pilot from Moscow.

Alexi was a skilled aviator and, one morning, took me up in the Hind to put her through its paces. He explained some of the combat maneuvers and I recall doing a "return to target" that almost certainly could have ended poorly. I couldn't help but notice that the Hind shook like a pig and that it was highly recommended that I strap down my boots to the leather pedals so that my feet wouldn't vibrate off. Most of the time, Galina flew the Hind along the route.

From North Dakota, I remember the route being south through South Dakota, Iowa, Cape Girardeau, Missouri, Alabama, central Florida (where we almost died near Zephyrhills in a hellacious thunderstorm), and finally into Miami's Watson Island.

FOUR: ANADYR FRIENDSHIP
Tony Trezciak

Made many trips to Anadyr, starting with the leaky hatch IL-62 flight in Jan. 1993. Shortly after arriving in Moscow, Aug. '92, I was assigned to be the coordinator for the first joint exercise with the Russian Air Force, Tiksi SAREX 93. Since the primary US players were assigned to Alaskan Air Command, there were USAF planning teams coming into Russia from Alaska and initially landing in Anadyr. I would accompany the teams to their destination as their interpreter, negotiator, USAF/Embassy representative, and whatever else to ensure both sides ended up with big smiles.

The exercise was a huge success, and the following year, ALCOM hosted a reciprocal exercise in Alaska. Again, this time as an escort and member of the Russian Air Force delegation, I ended up traversing Anadyr several more times.

To make a long story short, I got to know the Anadyr base commander, Col. Nikolay Kosteryev, quite well. We spent time ice fishing on the Anadyr Bay (salt water), transported by an MT-LB[82] tracked armored personnel carrier. I shocked the Moscow diplomatic community by taking leave and traveling with my family across Russia on Aeroflot at the invitation of Col. Kosteryev. Who in their right mind would spend leave time in Russia, take their family to Anadyr, and be hosted on a Russian Air Force base? Those were the days!

As an aside, I believe that I may have actually spent more time in the air flying with the Russian Air Force during those two years than in USAF aircraft in the previous seventeen years.

---

82. A Soviet multi-purpose, fully amphibious, tracked armored fighting vehicle in use since the 1970s.

I had an opportunity to ride in everything, from MI-8 helicopters to the AN-124. The IL-18 Coot VIP, with a separate section in the rear, was the usual transport when accompanying Russian Air Force senior staff from Moscow to various Russian Air Force Bases that we visited. Nice, smooth ride and great service! It was always an adventure!

FIVE: DOUBLE DUAL-ENGINE FLAMEOUTS
Colonel Chuck Miller, USAF (Ret.)

While going through some folders at home, I found the following flight summary from 1992 on the SU-27 fighter exchange. That flight into Grand Forks was nuts!

Summary of Escort Flight 92-53
To: LTC Westrom

The following is a summary of observations as flight escort aboard RU-78794 from Elmendorf AFB, AK, to Langley AFB, VA, and return.

I arrived at Elmendorf AFB on 10 July to act as escort aboard the IL-76, accompanied by two SU-27s, bound for Langley AFB as part of the First Fighter Exchange. The aircraft were due to arrive at Elmendorf on 11 July at about 1840Z (1040L). By 2030Z, there was still no word from the aircraft, nor had they been sighted by the radar at Adak, Alaska. I contacted the AF Operations Center to relay the delay and to see if they had an updated arrival time. No information was available from Ops or the FAA.

At 0130Z (1730L), I departed the base and began to check into a hotel for the night. I called the Command Post at Elmendorf to relay my location, and they informed me that the aircraft were 70 miles out. The aircraft landed, were serviced, and were ready to takeoff at about 0600Z. When asked about their delay, one crew member stated that they were only two hours late. He said the problem was getting customs in Anadyr, since the customs official was across the bay and there are no roads to the airport.

Aboard the aircraft, Commander Sergei Gorlov was helpful

and accommodating. The radio operator, Alexander Demenyshin (I believe), informed me that there was not an extra headset upstairs for me to monitor the radios with. The flight engineer reluctantly gave me his headset, but there was no means to transmit from his station (interphone only). I found this to be inadequate, since with my own headset and station, I could respond to ARTCC more quickly when the radio operator was unable, then translate the clearance or message. Without the ability to transmit, complex clearances would often take three or more transmissions to get across. The radio operator refused to listen to me for explanations or even simple things such as the correct frequency when he copied it incorrectly. It was a constant struggle to perform even the most basic part of my job.

After the first leg, I chose to ride downstairs in the navigator's bubble where I could have access to a headset with interphone readily accessible and all radios accessible by stepping next to the navigator and using his station. The instructor navigator, Alexander Bocharov, was very helpful and would give me free access to radios and interphone. It was Alexander who volunteered to give me his headset while he observed the younger navigator.

The younger navigator, Talgat Ramazanov (called Tolya), was very difficult to work with. When I would try to pass a correction to the radio operator upstairs, he would refuse to relay. If I needed to use the radios, he would first ask permission from the commander for the escort to use the radios. When I needed immediate access to the radios because of a clearance problem of misunderstanding by the radio operator, he would put his hand over the radio panel, denying me access to the radios, or he would push my hand out of the way. I explained that I must have immediate access to the radios to ensure flight safety and proper clearances, but to no avail.

The most congested times on interphone were when I needed access the most, and was often denied. This was partly due to the required coordination between the navigator and the rest of the crew, During the approach and landing phase, the crew would miss radio calls for altitudes or vectors due to the immense amount of interphone traffic, and I was unable to aid them.

The most dramatic time was when the SU-27s both had dual engine flameouts on their descent into Grand Forks AFB on their return trip. I was unable to contact ARTCC or the F-15 escort lead for several minutes because of the traffic on interplane and the junior navigator's continually pushing me away from the radio.

This is the story as I see it from both observation and from questioning the aircrews: Approximately 75 miles SE of Grand Forks AFB, passing FL 350, the two SU-27s experienced dual engine flameouts. The first, Tail #17 piloted by Alexander Kharchevski, obtained a relight almost immediately and lost little altitude. The second, Tail #62 piloted by Georgii Karabasov, fell behind the formation and lost altitude. I heard him say to the F-15 flight lead several times on interplane frequency "Georgii — two motors stop!" I listened to the radio and queried the navigator as to which engines on which aircraft didn't work. He explained and drew a picture stating that *both* aircraft had flamed out *both* engines, but wouldn't let me relay this to the F-15 lead (LTC Pelt), who assumed from Georgii's transmission that each aircraft had lost a single engine. The second SU-27 obtained a relight on one engine passing 12,000 ft MSL and restarted the second engine passing 6,000 ft MSL.

Recommendations:
  1. I need to (or Shotgun office) come up with a standardized briefing to the aircrews as to why we are riding with them and the importance of rapid radio

communications for flight safety. Although I emphasized this several times, maybe it needs to be in writing or submitted to the aircraft commander.
2. The Shotgun escort *must* have immediate access to radios and interphone, especially during the critical approach and landing phase.
3. The crews should be given an arrival and departure window. If they do not arrive or depart within this window, they should be turned back, fined, or made to sit for twelve to twenty-four hours. Six to ten hours late with no notification is unacceptable.
4. The crews need some sort of training on interphone discipline and not blocking radio calls. Crew coordination is severely lacking in the aircraft.

I hope this helps clear up some of the problems and conflicting stories encountered on this flight.

CHARLES F. MILLER, Major, USAF Constant Shotgun

After reading through the above flight summary, here's what I can add (in 2025):

Upon landing at Grand Forks, I told base ops to impound the aircraft (no service, nobody touches them) until we could figure out why the two fighters both suffered dual engine flameouts. Lt. Col. Pelt was less than helpful. I remember that he tried to pull rank, claimed that he was in charge of the flight, and generally just wanted to get the aircraft on their way. He was in charge of planning the exchange for Langley, and the successful mission would be a huge bonus for him on his way to Colonel.

After talking with both pilots, they admitted that they had not properly set their cockpit switches prior to descent and that when they pulled the throttles back from their cruise setting to begin descent, they inadvertently flamed out their engines (something to do with the fuel mix, but I'm not certain).

Once they had figured out that it was pilot error and not fuel contamination, I continued with servicing and we continued the mission to Langley.

When I was talking with the pilots about their flameouts, Alexander said that he had lost only a few thousand feet, that he was able to restart an engine right away and relight the other one while descending. Georgii wasn't as fortunate (or skilled). When I asked him how far he would descend before bailing out, he said that 3,000 feet was his minimum. I assume that this was 3,000 feet MSL, roughly 1,000 to 2,000 feet AGL, depending upon the terrain.

This is probably the closest we came to having a mishap, except for the Presidential support aircraft striking a windsock at Boeing Field. One other interesting note: The Russian crews significantly enriched my vocabulary of Russian obscenities with their frantic transmissions during the flameouts.

Many stories keep coming back ...

SIX: HURRICANE GLORIA & KGB POISON
Lieutenant Colonel Frank Peluso, USAF (Ret.)

In September 1985, we (Frank Peluso and Randy Elson) flew the regular Constant Shotgun mission in support of the UN General Assembly. As was the custom, we left the main party off at JFK, then flew the Aeroflot aircraft to Havana, Cuba, for several days. While we were in Cuba, we learned that Hurricane Gloria was forming in the Atlantic. When we flew back to JFK to pick up the dignitaries, the hurricane was gaining strength and threatening the East Coast. We knew we would not be able to fly out as scheduled.

After coordinating with Air Force Command Center (AFCC), we agreed that we should find a place to hunker down until the storm passed. AFCC made arrangements to fly the IL-62 to Scott AFB, Illinois. On hearing this, the Constant Shotgun crew suggested that was not a good idea, as Scott AFB had only a 7,000-foot runway. The Aeroflot crew agreed that they would prefer a longer runway.

AFCC reworked the problem and instructed us to fly to Little Rock AFB. The Aeroflot US representative (Mr. Agapov) insisted that we fly to Andrews first to pick up "embassy staff" to support the crew. By the time we got to Andrews AFB, it was already raining heavily. We flight planned, refueled, boarded the passengers, and departed for Little Rock. While on board, we noted that the Soviet Embassy staff included some familiar faces (i.e. people we knew were KGB), including Mr. Agapov himself.

We arrived at Little Rock, parked the airplane in a remote part of the base, and were taken to the VOQ (visiting officer quarters) to spend the night.

Early the next morning, I was awakened by a knock on the

door by a base OSI (Office of Special Investigations) officer. The OSI officer wanted to discuss how to handle the Aeroflot crew and their passengers. He indicated that some base personnel were being pressured to take the passengers on a grand tour of the base. I told him that as far as I was concerned, there was no protocol to cover this situation and there should be no negative ramifications if this request was denied. The OSI agent seemed relieved and agreed that he would not arrange such a tour.

Apparently, the OSI went back to their Russian guests and informed them that I had made the decision not to allow such a tour. I surmised this when later that morning, Mr. Agapov approached me and asked if I could arrange an "excursion" for him and his party. I answered with one word: "impossible." He immediately threw his hands up and backed off. The subject never came up again. (Note: Titan II missiles were stationed at Little Rock AFB. It did not take a rocket scientist to figure out that he and his "embassy support staff" saw this as an intelligence collection opportunity.)

Eventually, we continued on to New York, picked up the delegation, and departed for Moscow. As usual, once we were handed off to Moncton Center, we retired to the passenger cabin. We were served what we thought was the usual in-flight meal and beverages. After a short while, I began to feel ill. Eventually, this got worse, to the point that I was visiting the lavatory to vomit. Although the symptoms were severe, I managed to conceal my level of distress from the other passengers and crew. The symptoms lasted about six hours, then went away. I was feeling better by the time we arrived in Moscow.

I might have simply written my illness off as a mild case of food poisoning, but a similar short-term illness occurred on a subsequent flight to Moscow. Symptoms were consistent with the first incident. I later learned that one of our attachés in Moscow suffered the same type of incident. In his case, the Russians took embarrassing photographs of him in his incapacitated state.

Glossary & Acronyms

AB – Air Base
ADVON – ADVance EchelON; a team sent ahead of the main party to scope out the environment
AF – Air Force
AFB – Air Force Base (US)
AGL – Height Above Ground Level
ALCOM – Alaskan Command
ARTCC – Air Route Traffic Control Center, referred to as "Center" in pilot communications
ATC – Air Traffic Control; authorities responsible for the safe, orderly, and expeditious flow of air traffic. They direct pilots under IFR and guide and assist all pilots under both Instrument and Visual Flight Rules (VFR)
AUTOVON – Automatic Voice Network, a military long-distance telephone system used by the US from the 1960s to the 1990s
BX – Base Exchange; a military department store providing shopping services to USAF members on an AFB
Canuck – an endearing term for a Canadian citizen
Center – the common name for an ARTCC
CFB – Canadian Forces Base
CIA – The US Central Intelligence Agency (see KGB)
CIS – Commonwealth of Independent States (see FSU)
CODEL – Congressional Delegation
CONUS – Continental United States, sometimes called the Lower 48 (excludes Alaska and Hawaii)
DAVES – the airway intersection over the Atlantic east of Boston where our Shotgun duties usually began
DH – Decision Height; the lowest legal altitude allowed on a precision approach without visually acquiring the runway environment

DIA – Defense Intelligence Agency

DLAB – Defense Language Aptitude Battery; a test to determine a military member's overall propensity to learn any foreign language

DLI – Defense Language Institute; a master's level school in Monterrey, CA, where a multitude of foreign languages are taught full-time to military members entering a career field where foreign language proficiency is required

DLPT – Defense Language Proficiency Test; a test to gauge the level of proficiency in a specific foreign language; often, results of this test determined how much language pay is added to your monthly income

DoD – Department of Defense

FAA – Federal Aviation Administration, whose mission is to provide the safest, most efficient aerospace system in the world; they are the authority of all things aviation within the US

FBO – Fixed Base Operator (an airport's service station)

FL – Flight Level; at altitudes above 18,000' MSL, all aircraft set their altimeters to 29.92" of mercury, regardless of the actual barometric pressure. By knocking off two zeroes from the resultant altitude reading, 18,000' becomes FL180 and 35,000' becomes FL350

FOD – Foreign Object Damage; any loose object on the ground that might be sucked into a running engine or flipped into the air to strike an aircraft component

FPM – feet per minute; used to describe a climb or descent rate and displayed on a VSI or VVI

FSU – Former Soviet Union (Former USSR)

G – 1 force of gravity; pulling 2 G's would make everything in the aircraft weigh double its weight on earth

Go-Around – a VFR procedure that aborts a landing attempt

because of an unsafe situation, requiring the pilot to add power, climb, and proceed away from obstacles in order to circle back for a new attempt at a landing (see Missed Approach)

GPS – Global Positioning System

HF – High Frequency radio spectrum; used for long-distance radio communications (ham radio, for instance)

HSI – Horizontal Situation Indicator; a gyro compass in the cockpit that displays a bird's eye view of the aircraft's location in relation to a final approach course

HQ – Headquarters, as in HQ USAF at the Pentagon

Hypoxia – a lack of oxygen reaching the tissues of the body

ICAO – International Civil Aviation Organization; the worldwide authority that governs aviation rules and procedures; the equivalent to the FAA within the US

IFR – Instrument Flight Rules; flying without reference to the ground because of clouds; reference to avionic instrumentation is required (see VFR)

ILS – Instrument Landing System; ground-based navigational aid that provides both horizontal and vertical (glide slope) guidance

IMC – Instrument Meteorological Conditions ("in the clouds")

KGB – Комитет государственной безопасности, or The Committee for State Security; the Soviet Union's intelligence agency until 3 December 1991

L – Local Time versus Zulu Time

Lat/Long – Latitude & Longitude; coordinates to define a specific location on the map

Localizer – ground-based navigational aid that provides only horizontal positioning left or right of the runway centerline

Lt – Lieutenant

Mayday – the international call denoting life-threatening distress, usually repeated three times; a non-life-threatening situation could instead use the phrase 'Pan-Pan'

Medevac – Medical Evacuation flight to move patients

MIA – Missing in Action

MiG – Designation of an aircraft designed by Mikoyan, a Moscow-based aerospace company

Missed Approach – an aborted landing attempt under IFR (see Go-Around)

MDA – Minimum Descent Altitude; the legal limit to which you can descend on an instrument approach without visually acquiring the runway environment on a non-precision approach

MOA – Military Operations Area; designated airspace where flight training takes place, involving aerobatics, etc.

MSL – Altitude Above Mean Sea Level

MT-LB – *Mnogotselevoy tyagach legky bronirovanny*; a Soviet multi-purpose, fully amphibious, tracked armored fighting vehicle in use since the 1970s

Non-Precision Approach – an instrument procedure where only lateral guidance is provided by a ground-based navigational aid (NAVAID); that is, there is no vertical guidance, such as a glide slope indication

NATO – North American Treaty Organization

NAVAID – a navigational aid that provides electronic course and/or glide slop information; these can be either space-based (such as GPS) or ground-based (such as VORTAC)

NDB – Non-Directional Beacon, an old WW2 ground-based navigational aid

NM – Nautical Mile, or 6,000 feet

NORAD – North American Air Defense

NW – Northwest

O-6 – Officer, pay grade 6, which is a full Colonel

OSI – USAF Office of Special Investigations

Pan Am – PanAmerican Airlines (out of business 1991)

PAX – Nickname referring to "passengers"

PCA – Positive Controlled Airspace; antecedent to what was changed to Class A airspace in September 1993; consisting of altitudes from FL180 to FL600

Phonetic Alphabet – words used to denote letters of the alphabet clearly over the radio, e.g. "Alpha," "Bravo," or "Charlie"

PIC – Pilot-in-Command; legally responsible for the safe operation of the flight; at any one time, there can only be one PIC even though there may be other pilots on board

POW/MIA – Prisoner of War / Missing in Action

Precision Approach – an instrument procedure that provides both lateral and vertical guidance to assist in bringing an aircraft into a landing position through IMC

RAF – Royal Air Force (Britain)

RO – Radio Operator; a position on an aircrew with the sole responsibility to communicate with ATC; should be a good English speaker, as English is the universal language of aviation worldwide

Rubles – standard monetary unit in the USSR; uses the symbol ₽

SAREX – Search and Rescue Exercise

SM – Statute Mile, or 5,280 feet; the standard mile measured on roads in the US

Squawk – Aviation slang for a four-digit transponder code that uniquely identifies a specific aircraft for controller's use

START – Strategic Arms Reduction Treaty, signed by US President George H.W. Bush and USSR General Secretary Mikhail Gorbachev

TIME – International flight requires the use of Universal Time, commonly known as "Zulu." Throughout this book, a four-digit military time annotation is used, such that 1300L means

Local time, and 1300Z means Zulu time; 0630Z should be pronounced "oh-six-thirty Zulu"

TLAR – "That Looks About Right"; an educated operational guess made by an experienced pilot

UB – Учебно-Боевой; the designation for the two-seat Combat Trainer version of a Soviet aircraft; the front seat being for the student and the rear for the instructor

UHF – Ultra High Frequency radio spectrum (used extensively by military aircraft)

UN – United Nations

USAF – United States Air Force

USSR – Union of Soviet Socialist Republics; originally included the modern countries of Azerbaijan, Belarus, Estonia, Georgia, Kazakhstan, Kyrgyzstan, Latvia, Lithuania, Moldova, Russia, Tajikistan, Turkmenistan, Ukraine, and Uzbekistan

VFR – Visual Flight Rules; must maintain visual contact with the ground at all times (see IFR)

VHF – Very High Frequency radio spectrum, used mainly by civilian aircraft

VIP – Very Important Person

VOQ – Visiting Officer Quarters

VOR – VHF Omnidirectional Rangefinder, a ground-based navigational aid for aircraft

VSI – Vertical Speed Indicator, which displays climb or descent rates in FPM

VVI – Vertical Velocity Indicator; another name for VSI

VVS – военно-воздушные силы, Soviet Military Air Forces

XO – often means Executive Officer, but is also an office symbol for the Operations Directorate of HQ USAF at the Pentagon

Z – Zulu Time; the common nickname for what was called Greenwich Mean Time until 1928; in today's official vernacular, it is called UTC, or Universal Time Coordinated

www.ingramcontent.com/pod-product-compliance
Lightning Source LLC
Chambersburg PA
CBHW050337010526
44119CB00049B/588